Big Bully

BIG BULLY

An Epidemic of Unkindness

Marion Scher

BOOK**STORM**

ISBN: 978-1-77995-009-3
e-ISBN: 978-1-77995-010-9

First edition, first impression 2023

Published by Bookstorm (Pty) Ltd
PO Box 4532
Northcliff 2115
Johannesburg
South Africa
www.bookstorm.co.za

Edited by Russell Clarke
Proofread by Janet Bartlet
Cover design by Dogstar Design
Typesetting by Liquid Type Publishing Services
Printed in the USA

To all those who don't step away when
they see someone being bullied.

And to my family, who constantly support me
in everything I do – a massive thank you.

CONTENTS

FOREWORD

"Without mental health there can be no true physical health" is a well-known adage from Dr Brock Chisholm, the first director-general of the World Health Organization (WHO). These 10 words, indicating the irrevocable link between mental and physical health, are often quoted and are true for every single living person, for how can you be healthy when one part of your body is suffering?

Over the past few years, much has been done to raise awareness and decrease stigma around conditions that affect the brain. Depression, anxiety, bipolar disorder and attention deficit hyperactivity disorder (ADHD) are no longer taboo words, whispered softly under our breath. They are discussed openly, education campaigns have been embarked upon, and many celebrities have stepped up to the plate and spoken out about their own experiences – going further to instil the notion that "it's okay not to be okay".

A topic, however, which has received virtually no airtime is that of bullying. The word bullying conjures up an image of a child being taunted on a playground. And yet bullying encompasses so much more than that, and the many consequences of bullying are far reaching. In addition, in the world we live in today, bullying is relentless. Children, adolescents and young adults in a tertiary setting are no longer able to escape the learning environment for a brief respite at home. Social media is omnipotent and so the bullying continues, day and night. It's no wonder the statistics are showing increased rates of suicide in relation to bullying and cyberbullying.

In this book, another important topic is covered – bullying in the workplace. A tough concept to grasp because adults *should* behave like adults, and the workplace *should* be a place of productivity, differing opinions and working towards one common goal. But often, workplace bullying is the exact opposite and far more insidious than schoolyard bullying. It is also virtually never reported, of which the bully is fully cognizant. Yet the dichotomy exists: whilst one's self worth is continually eroded, and the culture of fear predominates, victims need the security a job offers and feel unable to speak up.

Lastly, home is not always a safe haven for everyone. You'll read about the fear that grips a person when they hear a garage or front door being opened, knowing abuse will soon follow. Emotional abuse leaves deep, lingering scars.

This book was partially made possible through a donation from our company, Lundbeck. Lundbeck is a Danish pharmaceutical company, specialising in medications for psychiatric and neurological disorders. Over the years, we have enjoyed a special partnership with the South African Depression and Anxiety Group (SADAG) to offer support to the lifesaving projects they embark upon. This phenomenal group of people work tirelessly to improve the lives of those suffering from mental illness. In the hope we can play a small part, we offer contributions on an annual basis.

Our support for this book is no different. We are proud to be affiliated with SADAG, and commend the work undertaken to produce this eye-opening account of bullying across the spectrum of people's lives. Our donation is in the form of an unrestricted grant, which means we have a hands-off approach, leaving the experts to do what they know best!

Every morning, every employee in our organisation wakes up and makes sure "we are tirelessly dedicated to restoring brain health, so every person can be their best". We live by our motto, we breathe it and we sleep it, and we are grateful for the opportunity to support this initiative.

Team Lundbeck South Africa

INTRODUCTION

When I wrote my last book, *Surfacing: People Coping with Depression and Mental Illness*, one topic cropped up time after time in the personal stories featured in the book – bullying. There's no time limit on bullying, and contrary to what many people think bullying doesn't just occur at school. It's rampant and affects every member of society from crèche to retirement. And it's getting worse, not better, with very few people willing to talk or do something about it. Similar to mental health issues, bullying is a topic that needs to be talked about – now more than ever we need a dose of positivity, we need people to "be nice"...

Making people aware of being nice isn't a new idea to me. A number of years ago, I was working for a radio station that ran very successful campaigns motivating South Africans to "Stand up, do the right thing, and lead by example." I suggested running a "be nice" campaign. Something simple, like encouraging people to say please and thank you to anyone who offers a service, from a cashier at a supermarket till, to a petrol station attendant or a waitron. Sadly, the campaign never happened – but the idea of simply teaching people to be nice has never left me. Instead of a snide remark, leaving someone out of something or being downright nasty, how can we instil niceness in people, and maybe help stop bullying?

As with the planning of any book, there had to be a clear conception of just which areas of bullying would be covered and although bullying has no limits of age, race, culture or social standing, I chose the areas of teens, the workplace, relationships and social media. These cover almost every aspect of bullying, from the subtle to the insidious. When it came to funding I knew, through the work they do in the field of mental health worldwide, that Lundbeck would be the perfect partner for such a book, which they truly have been.

For the last 28 years much of my writing has been around mental health awareness and wellness, hoping to help lessen the stigma around these topics. With bullying often being the root of future mental health problems, this book was a natural progression for me. As a contributor and columnist to most of South Africa's top publications over the years, I learnt that whenever I did a story that touched on mental health issues, I would get an immediate response from people who were desperate to know they weren't on their own in such battles. It didn't take long into my initial research to discover what an enormous and mostly uphill battle people were facing with bullying in every sphere of life. There is also a large body of research on which to draw, plus wonderful experts who were only too happy to offer their time and expertise to the creation of this book.

Before I could write a single word about bullying, though, I needed to find people willing to talk to me. I put out messages on social media calling on individuals to contact me should they wish to talk about their experiences. As I've done in the past, I used my own friend and colleague network to seek out case studies. People who had been bullied, their families, and, I was hoping, the bullies themselves. What I discovered was that very few people, if any, would admit to being a bully. I was initially a little disappointed with the responses to this request, although those I did receive came from a broad cross section of South African society. Those individuals who had been bullied did talk to me, although it was often really hard for them, and their stories will ring true for many of you.

By the time I finished writing this book I realised that for many or even most bullies, this is just the way they ride – this is how they've been socialised and operate in the world. Most would, in fact, be horrified to hear themselves described as a bully. They see themselves either as the cool dude or top girl, or the boss who has to maintain control of his or her unruly staff, or the husband whose wife expects nothing less than his full attention.

I really hope some of these people read *Big Bully* and see themselves mirrored in its pages. Indeed, when I mentioned to people that I was researching and writing this book, the general reaction was that a fresh look at bullying is really needed, and would I please make sure that schools, companies and South Africans in general read the book and take note. I sincerely hope they do. Although there has been much written on this topic previously, this is an evolving subject, with bullies no less affected by the latest technology than anyone else – and using it to its fullest advantage.

According to a recent UNICEF report, on average South Asia and West and Central Africa experience the most bullying, while countries from Central and Eastern Europe and the Eurasian Commonwealth of Independent States (CEE/CIS) experience the least. African countries – including Botswana, Ghana, South Africa, Egypt and Zambia – are the most common in the top ten countries with the highest bullying rates.[1]

Perhaps I was more aware of bullying during the early stages of researching this book when I happened to go to lunch at a restaurant within a bowling club, popular with families. Whilst sitting there enjoying watching children of all ages running wild on the bowling green, my attention was caught by one particular little boy. He couldn't have been more than 20 months old and the group of children around him ranged from two to six years old. Not one of these children was spared from his behaviour, whether it was hitting, kicking or pulling hair – with each child running off in tears. After around 30 minutes of this brutality, his mother finally appeared to drag him off to the family's table. As she sat down with him she was rewarded with a mighty (for a little guy) slap to her face. Her reaction was to speak to him, but they were too far away for me to overhear the conversation.

The point is, was this a "one off"? I doubt it. What I saw could be the beginning of the life of a bully. One where the child would possibly grow into a schoolboy aware of what power he could wield through his own strength. Assuming there would be no intervention, chances are that this would see him develop into an adult, a boss, a husband or a father whose bullying impacts the lives of those around him. In his lifetime, his actions could possibly affect the mental and physical health of numerous people who might cross his path, leaving indelible marks on each of them.

The situation described above, particularly given that this toddler's language skills were minimal, was physical bullying. But make no mistake, verbal bullying is as destructive, if not more so, than the physical form. The old idiom of "Sticks and stones may break my bones, but words can never hurt me" is aptly reinterpreted here by Brendan Byrne:

> Sticks and stones may break my bones,
> but words can also hurt me.
> Stones and sticks break only skin,
> while words are ghosts that haunt me.
> Slant and curved the word-swords fall,
> to pierce and stick inside me.
> Bats and bricks may ache through bones,
> but words can mortify me.
> Pain from words has left its scar,
> on mind and heart that's tender.
> Cuts and bruises now have healed,
> it's words that I remember.[2]

Referring to words as "ghosts that haunt me" will ring true in many readers' minds when they reflect on words that may have been said to them over the years, never truly leaving their psyche. The same goes for "words can mortify me". In *Big Bully*, you'll read people's own stories of just how they were mortified and worse, often in front of other people, by bullies. By words uttered perhaps by relatives, partners or bosses, that have not only stuck with them through life, but impinged on their whole outlook on life and how they see themselves. Needless to say, often leading to mental health issues.

In case you're wondering why, when I've just mentioned how even toddlers can bully, you'll find no other mention of small children in these pages, it is because the topic merits an entire book of its own. You can't, however, get around the fact that how parents deal with bullying behaviour in small children will impact not just on whether they become bullies themselves – but how they handle such behaviour as adolescents and adults.

According to the UNESCO Institute of Statistics, one-third of the globe's youth is bullied: this ranges from as low as 7% in Tajikistan to 74% in Samoa. Low socioeconomic status is a main factor in youth bullying within wealthy countries, and immigrant-born youth in wealthy countries are more likely to be bullied than locally-born youth.[3]

The school bully

If you got through your school career without ever encountering one of these sadistic kids, you can count yourself a rarity. Even if they weren't in your face, you knew they were there; and if you were clever, you avoided them. In my case, the bullies were the sixth form girls at an all-girls school, who felt that because they'd gone through these terrors when they were new girls, it was their time to inflict pain on the newbies and ensure the cycle continued. When I look back, it's hard to imagine how they got away with their abusive behaviour, given that it was perpetrated in broad daylight with teachers around every turn. But they did. You were punished for small things such as stepping onto the grass in the courtyards (as this was sixth-form holy territory), which in itself isn't such a big deal – but when you're made to do penance for this, it becomes an issue.

In many boys' schools the situation is far worse, as we see when an incident blows up as a front-page story. Bullying can take the form of being made to run up and down rows of seats in a sports pavilion in over 30-degree heat, or far more humiliating, hitting or beating a boy whilst simultaneously filming the abuse to share with others. This very incident happened as I write this, in a Gauteng school, with the child sustaining a concussion from the violent beating. The school's reaction when his father complained was suspension for those involved, but the perpetrators will return to school and the pupil will be forced once again to face them.

I contacted a number of schools for their thoughts and input into this book, and received no responses except for one outstanding and therefore highly mentionable school, Westerford High School in Cape Town. Both the headmaster and deputy head went to great lengths, not only to give me their insights on the topic, but also to arrange for me to speak to a group of their students. The refusal of schools to talk about bullying says it all. Not admitting to or discussing the problem means they don't have a problem, which I quickly discovered is a total impossibility, particularly in the cyber age of social media and networking.

School bullying in South Africa:

- More than 3.2 million learners are bullied yearly in South Africa.
- More than 67% of bullying victims will not ask a teacher for help because they don't think it will change their situation.
- 90% of school bullying is carried out by learners.
- 1 in 10 learners drop out of school to avoid being bullied.
- 16% of learners admit that they are victims of cyberbullying.[4]

The workplace bully

When I asked for people to talk to me about their experiences of workplace bullying, I was inundated with responses. It almost seems normal to expect to find at least one or two bullies in your place of employment. The stories I was told ranged from bosses whose demands were way outside the parameters of the job – with the ongoing threat of being fired held over an employee's head – to the grown-up version of the school bully, whose aim was simply to make another person's life as miserable as possible. And with a weak economy and fewer jobs to choose from compounding the situation, it seems the bullies have free rein.

In a surprising twist, women bosses in particular came out at the top of the horror stakes of workplace bullies, with many people telling me they would never want to work for a woman again. The common thread here, which the experts I interviewed all confirmed, was that these bullies were repeating actions that they themselves had undergone, or that they thought were normal.

The relationship bully

I had to brace myself to hear the often heartbreaking and vicious stories from those who encountered torturous relationships. The big question I kept asking myself was, "How could you get involved with such a person?" But just who is that kind of person, and is it even possible to spot them? When you do realise that your relationship may not be a bed of roses, how easy is it to get away from your partner-bully? These are the questions you probably want answered, either to understand this type of bullying or to realise that you could also possibly be trapped in this type of relationship.

The cyberbully

With technology becoming so intimately intertwined with our daily lives, it's not surprising that we're seeing a drastic increase in cyberbullying. This situation was further exacerbated by the Covid-19 pandemic and its associated lockdowns, forcing people to spend more time online and exposing them to the risks of bullying and worse. Paedophiles came out of the woodwork eager to find new prey to lure into their vile networks. As I finished writing this book, Covid-19 had become far less of a threat, but the growth in online exposure hasn't.

The experts

No book on such a topic would be complete without the insight of those who deal with such subjects on a daily basis and *Big Bully* is no different. You'll read feedback from some of South Africa's leading experts in this field, offering advice on just how to cope with the insidious social ill of bullying.

I am greatly indebted to all the experts who took the time and effort to contribute to this book and help you, the reader, understand not just why someone bullies but also how to deal with these situations. Most I have interviewed over the years, confident in their ability to be able to give expert opinions everyone can understand, as well as having faith in their skills. As always, SADAG were invaluable in securing interviews with experts, as well as some case studies.

You'll be hearing from the following people in the coming pages:

Ronald Addinall is a clinical social worker and lecturer at the University of Cape Town. Addinall is also a sexologist and academic with 29 years' professional practice experience across many fields in social work, and has a special interest in human sexuality and gender nonconformity.

Paul Channon is the former headmaster of The Ridge School, and a leading educationalist. Channon is the director of the Alexandra Education Committee, which seeks to provide excellent educational and psychosocial support for school children from disadvantaged backgrounds in and around Alexandra township.

Ilana Gerschlowitz is a former lawyer, parent-coach and expert on autistic spectrum disorder (ASD). She is also the founder and director of The Star Academy, a centre for autism education, as well as being an author and mother of three children, two of whom were diagnosed with autism.

Cayley Jorgensen is a registered counsellor with the Health Professions Council of South Africa. She is also the director of FaceUp South Africa, an anti-corruption, well-being and child protection platform. FaceUp is an international organisation that not only creates a safe space for learners to report bullying and other challenges, but also helps schools and companies put plans in place to improve these situations.

Dr Ruwayne Kock is an executive coach and registered organisational psychologist who works as a practitioner and academic. He is a member of Coaches and Mentors of South Africa (COMENSA) and also serves on the management and executive committee of the Society of Industrial and Organisational Psychology of South Africa (SIOPSA).

Luke Lamprecht has three decades of experience working in the non-profit and child protection sector. Lamprecht works with children in conflict with the law, with autism, with behavioural challenges and psychiatric diagnoses, as well as children in mainstream schooling. He is an expert consultant on child protection and development, sexual abuse and toxic masculinity.

Ian Lipman is a clinical psychologist who practices in Johannesburg, and specialises in relationship counselling.

Liane Lurie is a registered clinical psychologist, with a particular interest in working with adolescents. She runs school-based programmes for parents, teachers and learners focused on areas such as bullying, self-harm and eating disorders.

Joshna Lutchman is a social worker and is the head of operations and training at The Family Life Centre of South Africa (FAMSA) in Johannesburg.

Dean McCoubrey has been an expert in traditional, digital and social media for over 20 years, as well being a parent of teens and pre-teens. He is the founder of MySocialLife, an organisation that offers digital life skills and media literacy training to young people. McCoubrey works closely with schools and parents, and trains clinical psychologists, general practitioners and school counsellors.

Vanessa Richards is a social worker in Johannesburg specialising in child, adolescent and adult psychotherapy, with a particular interest in parenting plans.

Professor Renata Schoeman has been a psychiatrist dealing with children, adolescents and adults since 2008. She's also an associate professor at Stellenbosch Business School. Prof Schoeman is on the advisory boards of various pharmaceutical companies and is the convenor of the South African Society of Psychiatrists' (SASOP) special interest group for adult ADHD. She is a co-founder and director of the Goldilocks and The Bear Foundation, a non-profit organisation that offers free ADHD and mental health screening, and early intervention services in underprivileged communities.

Dr Renate Volpe is an expert in the field of strategic leadership and people development. Volpe has experience in the world of business and academia, as well as being a well-known public speaker, life coach and entrepreneur. She has spent the last 20 years specialising in women's development and is the co-author of *Senseless Sacrifice: Givers and Takers in Relationships.*

The stories

When it comes to the stories you're about to read, every word appears just as related by the people who chose to share their experiences with me and you, the reader. Although it wasn't easy getting people to come forward with their stories, social media sites such as Twitter, LinkedIn and Facebook offered valuable platforms to find these people. As this book was partly written during the Covid-19 pandemic, not all interviews were face to face; some were conducted online through Zoom or Microsoft Teams. Many, though, were in person. Either way, it was impossible for the emotion of each story not to show and even through a screen, the pain was palpable.

I'm sure you will understand why we have chosen not to use the respondents' real names. An asterisk* indicates where a name has been changed. The fear of repercussion is very real with such stories, and for that reason I have respected the request for anonymity. I want to sincerely thank each and every person who opened their hearts and souls to share what was a painful chapter of their lives. Just know that your story will help so many others.

CHAPTER 1

What is bullying?

FOR MANY OF US, when we hear the word bully we think of the movie version of the schoolyard bully. The loud-mouthed tough kid, bigger than average and feared by everyone except those in his immediate group, and possibly other bullies, or those who just want to hang out with the cool guys. But you'd be wrong – very wrong. Bullies come in all shapes and sizes, and even family can be your worst nightmare, not to mention partners or your own children. And a word about the "he" pronoun – not so much, as I pointed out in the introduction – it turns out women can be as bad, if not worse, bullies than men.

According to clinical psychologist Liane Lurie, "With boy bullies it's generally more physical acts of aggression, while with girls it's far more insidious. They'll often create a behind-the-scenes undercurrent that's difficult for the victim to put their finger on, but they know something's not right. It could be that a girl hears some friends had a party on Saturday night and she wasn't invited. She thinks hard before confronting her 'friend', but eventually questions why she wasn't invited to the party. The other girl is going to say, 'No, there wasn't a party, it was just two of us – we had a sleepover.' Now the victim feels ashamed because she thinks perhaps she was imagining things – but was she? Highly unlikely. When you don't approve of something, or the other person won't acknowledge fault, the only tangible person you have is yourself and so you take all that blame, turn it inward and think you must be responsible, and that you did something wrong to deserve this," explains Lurie.

Most of us have experienced that feeling of exclusion at some time and can identify with the "left out" syndrome. The same girl bully might grow up and go on to be the petite lady who sits at the next desk to you, and whilst she'll appear to be all smiles and good advice, behind your back she's spreading rumours about you, which could cause more harm than an actual knife in your back.

I mention families above, and yes, here I'm talking about mothers and fathers. What, you ask – how could parents be bullies?

Parents are often the first bullying experience people have, impacting heavily on their lives. Can you imagine being told on a regular basis from a very young age that you're useless, unlikely to amount to anything, always in the way, and worse?

For Winston*, "Home was a lot more of a mental game. Firstly, I wasn't the strongest person there. My sister was tougher and sportier than me, which I was aware of from the age of five. I was the complete opposite and tried to avoid all the things she loved – roller coasters and base jumping. This was fodder for my family who were constantly pointing out my weaknesses, telling me I wasn't strong enough, which just led me to believe that I was a weak person. It wasn't my mom so much, but my father and sister were like a gang on their own – with me always being out of step with them. The words 'toughen up' were my father's mantra for me. Occasionally he'd say he loved me, but words only go so far. I never had that feeling of connection, that I could actually go and hug him. Somehow I never felt worthy, or that I'd ever reach any goals, or succeed. I was desperately missing that family support."

If we spoke to Winston's family about how he felt they would probably look puzzled, as if we were talking about a stranger and not their son and brother. Sometimes, family are so close to you and become so familiar, you don't realise the impact of your words and actions on them. As far as they're concerned, they're toughening you up for the real world: "Life is tough – you need to get used to it"; "There are no free handouts – you have to earn respect/love/kindness". But do you? Especially as a child who simply wants to know that, if nothing else, they have their family's support and love. Yes, the world is a tough place, but that doesn't mean you need to get used to abuse at home.

When it comes to brutality, words can do far more harm than a punch. The worst and most damaging abuse is often verbal. Words can't be unsaid and will often haunt a person's life forever, whereas a broken bone can heal. This is where the traditional image of the bully falls away. A bully doesn't fit into any one particular physical mould, so it's impossible to spot one visually. Research shows that in fact, most bullies are intelligent, popular and highly charismatic.[5] They could also be angry, aggressive, hyperactive and even violent, but this is often just under the surface where not everyone is allowed to look.

Janet's* ex-husband was a well-known figure in the world of sport, as well as a successful professional in his field. She'd met him at high school and by the time they both went to university he'd made it clear that she was a permanent part of his life then, and in the future. They went to different universities, hundreds of kilometres apart, but each night at 9 pm she had to be at the call box on campus (in the days before cell phones) to answer his nightly check-in. Or should I say check-up?

"If I wasn't able to take his call, he wanted to know why. It wasn't overt but gave me a sense that I had to be there," explains Janet. "I'm a people pleaser by nature, so this was the beginning of our relationship being on his terms. What this meant was while all my fellow students were enjoying themselves in clubs and societies or just hanging out at night, I couldn't do that. I had to take that call at 9 pm." What Janet wasn't able to foresee then was that this would be the pattern of her future married life, where her husband became a celebrity in his field and she ignored her real career path to stay home and attend to mothering duties. Janet describes him as being a classic narcissist.

After you read this book, you'll understand that whilst there are many forms of bullying, the common link is a form of abuse, with nearly every person I interviewed describing their particular bully as being narcissistic. So what is a **narcissist?**

According to the American Psychological Association, someone with a **narcissistic personality disorder** (NPD) has the following characteristics: (a) a long-standing pattern of grandiose self-importance and an exaggerated sense of talent and achievements; (b) fantasies of unlimited sex, power, brilliance or beauty; (c) an exhibitionistic need for attention and admiration; (d) either cool indifference or feelings of rage, humiliation or emptiness as a response to criticism, indifference or defeat; and (e) various interpersonal disturbances, such as feeling entitled to special favours, taking advantage of others, and inability to empathise with the feelings of others.[6]

Psychiatrist Professor Renata Schoeman points out that you can't talk about bullying without talking about abuse. "**Abuse** is any form of behaviour that instils fear in a victim, causing emotional, physical or financial damage to someone, or coercing victims into doing something against their will such as taking part in sexual activities."

abuse: treat with cruelty or violence, especially regularly or repeatedly.

There are some forms of abusive behaviour that are not visible, but rather bullying by omission, explains Schoeman. "It could be the subtle withholding of care, support and finances. Often in close relationships, it's difficult to know whether you're being abused, especially if your partner says they love you, gives you a lot of attention, or pays for groceries or rent – yet instils fear or emotional trauma through their actions or words."

Over the years of writing stories about abuse, I've seen the same patterns emerge time after time, with the same comments: "I wanted to leave, but didn't know how." Very often children play a role here, and whether for financial or emotional reasons, we historically see couples stick it out through a bad marriage.

"And it's not just the controlling romantic partner, but also the intimidating boss or colleague, the difficult neighbour, the pushy sales rep, the condescending family member or social acquaintance or friend who shames you," says Schoeman. "**Bullying** is a deliberate act with the purpose of harming another – through power to instil fear, victimisation, or harassment. A bully, male or female, gains power in a relationship by reducing another's, and shows little regard for the consequences to a victim's health or well-being. Bullying is abuse!"

> **bullying:** a deliberate act seeking to harm, intimidate or coerce someone perceived as vulnerable.

The many types of abuse

Prof Schoeman describes the following types of abuse, all of which will be expanded on in the coming chapters:

Physical abuse

Physical abuse is any intentional act causing injury, trauma, bodily harm or other physical suffering to another person or animal by way of bodily contact. This can include scratching, punching, biting, strangling or kicking you; throwing something at you (a phone or a shoe); pulling or pushing you around; the use of weapons; grabbing your face to force you to look at them; grabbing you to prevent you from leaving; or forcing you to go somewhere.

Verbal or emotional abuse

Verbal abuse involves using spoken words, written words and gestures directed at a victim in order to scare or intimidate them. It can also include even just the threat of someone hurting you or your loved ones, including your pets. This may not cause physical damage, but does cause long lasting emotional pain and scarring. Verbal abuse can also easily escalate to physical violence. Constantly being criticised and told you aren't good enough causes you to lose confidence and lowers your self-esteem. In a relationship, you may actually start believing what your partner says (for example, that you're ugly, worthless or useless). As a result, you may start to blame yourself for your partner's abusive behaviour. Emotional abuse in a relationship includes controlling behaviour, such as isolating you from family and friends; monitoring what you're doing and where you are throughout the day; demanding your passwords; deciding for you what you should wear; extreme jealousy, including constant accusations of cheating; having a quick temper (and then blaming you for the outburst); and demeaning and belittling you. Emotional bullying is also common in the workplace, and can include gossiping or starting rumours about a person or a group of individuals.

Non-verbal abuse

Instead of using words to frighten or intimidate, glares and stares are used. When just one look is enough to reduce you to a state of anxiety or fear, or the silent treatment is used to manipulate you.

Sexual abuse

This refers to any action that pressures or coerces someone to do something sexually that they don't want to do. It can also refer to behaviour that impacts a person's ability to control their sexual activity or the circumstances in which it occurs, including oral sex, rape or restricting access to birth control and condoms. It's important to know that just because the victim didn't say no, it doesn't mean they meant yes. When someone doesn't resist an unwanted sexual advance, it doesn't mean they consented. Sometimes, physical resistance can put a victim at more risk for further physical or sexual abuse.

Racial, cultural and religious abuse

This involves being picked on or singled out solely on the basis that someone is "different" from others in their group, class or workplace.

Financial abuse

Financial abuse happens most often in intimate relationships, and occurs when one person has control over another's access to economic resources. It can be very subtle, such as giving you an allowance and monitoring closely how you spend it; placing your salary in their account and denying you access; using your credit card without permission; keeping you from accessing shared bank accounts or financial records; controlling the number of hours you're allowed to work, or making it impossible to go to work (by taking your car or keys); creating havoc at work (by harassing you or your co-workers); withholding necessities such as money, food, rent, medicine or clothing; using funds from joint accounts without your knowledge; or using their money to hold power over you because they know you're not in the same financial position as they are.

Technological abuse

Also known as cyberbullying, this is the use of digital technologies such as messaging and social networking to bully, harass, stalk or intimidate another person or partner. Often this behaviour is a form of verbal or emotional abuse – but online. Examples include someone sending, posting or sharing negative, harmful, false or mean content about you or to you; controlling who you're allowed to befriend or not on social media sites; negative, insulting or threatening messages sent via cell phone or email; stealing your passwords; constantly texting you and making you feel like you can't be separated from your phone for fear you'll be punished; or using technology (such as spyware or GPS in a car or on a phone) to monitor you and your movements.

Institutionalised bullying

This form of abuse occurs when various types of bullying become an accepted norm in a school, workplace or institution. This could be initiations at schools or sports clubs, as well as within organisations or institutions like universities and colleges.

Stalking

Stalking is when a person repeatedly watches, follows or harasses you, making you feel afraid or unsafe, and is another type of abuse. A stalker can be someone you know, a former partner, or a stranger. Stalkers may show up at your home or place of work unannounced or uninvited; send you unwanted text messages, letters, emails and voicemails; leave unwanted items, gifts or flowers; spread rumours about you via the internet or by word of mouth; or even damage your home, car or other property.

Who is a prime target for a bully?

Although many victims will tell you they think they might have done something to cause the bullying they experienced, this is obviously not true. I heard over and over again during interviews that people felt, initially at least, that they were to blame for what was happening to them, whilst bullying is really about the bad choices bullies make and not a defect in the victim. This is why, when a parent tells their child that bullying is a part of growing up and will make them stronger, they need to realise they're giving their child license to believe they deserve to be bullied, whether as a child or an adult.

Very few of us are born with great self-confidence; we rely on other people to contribute to this, particularly our families when we're young and haven't yet come up against life's hardships. We don't know who we are or what we're made of at this point in our lives. Experts feel that this is one of the reasons people like belonging to groups that make them part of something good, the opposite of what a bully wants them to feel – like outcasts and outsiders.

You have to have self-confidence in spades not to internalise bullies' negative messages and see yourself as a failure. Unfortunately, it's at this point that depression and anxiety can set in, often accompanied by unacted upon anger and rage. Universally, research clearly points out that a good social support network can drastically affect a bullying victim's short- and long-term outcomes. A supportive family, friends and peers that a person feels they can trust and talk to, who will listen and offer support and advice, can lessen the impact of bullying.

Bullying is also often something we expect to go through at school – almost a rite of passage – but research shows the results of childhood bullying puts people at risk in adulthood, not just for psychological health problems causing depression and anxiety, but also for compromised physical health, cognitive functioning and ultimately their quality of life. The end result, as I've seen and heard during my research, often being suicidal ideation (thoughts or ideas of suicidal behaviour), with cyberbullying increasingly being cited as a large and growing part of the problem.

Who is likely to be bullied?

Anyone remotely different from their peer groups or families are more likely to be made targets of bullying. People who fall into the following categories are particularly at risk:

- Children and adults with developmental delays.
- Anyone struggling with low self-esteem.
- Those who experience learning difficulties, or have physical or cognitive impairments.
- Those on the autism spectrum.
- People who suffer from social awkwardness or social anxiety.

- Minority groups – this could be based on religion, ethnicity, race and class.
- Those who are shy, submissive or socially isolated.
- People who are anxious or depressed.
- People who struggle with body issues, such as being overweight.
- Those who identify or present as LGBTQIA+ (lesbian, gay, bisexual, transgender, queer or questioning, intersex, asexual, and many other gender and sexual identities).

When does teasing become bullying?

Whether at school or at home, being teased by your peers or your family can leave its mark. There's a very fine line between **teasing** and bullying – laughing with, and laughing at. Very often the person that's doing the teasing will suffer from social awkwardness themselves, and feel that by teasing another person, they're dealing with their own issues. The *Cambridge Dictionary* definition of teasing is "to intentionally annoy a person or animal by saying something that is not true or pretending to do something, often in a playful way".[7] This is totally accurate because generally when you ask a bully to explain their behaviour, their response will be "I was only teasing."

> **teasing:** intentionally annoy a person or animal by saying something that is not true or pretending to do something, often in a playful way.

When interviewed, it was amazing to discover just how many people remember incidents of overt teasing, years after the events occurred. They leave a strong mark and some people even told me how they could never again have a relationship with a family member, such as a sibling, who constantly teased or bullied them as a child. Perhaps it's a case of when teasing loses its humorous edge and results in humiliation and loss of self-respect for the person on the receiving end.

Whilst technology has generally changed lives for the better, one of the areas of its impact that's had negative results has been cyberbullying, in young people's lives and right up to the elderly. I heard cases of 11- and 12-year-old girls sending nude photos of themselves to so-called boyfriends who, either whilst in the relationship or after it breaks up, will share these images with the excuse that "they're just bragging about what their girlfriend sent them".

These are the types of stories Cayley Jorgensen, counsellor and director at FaceUp South Africa, hears all the time. FaceUp goes into schools to try and help with cyberbullying but sees the same major problem at almost every school. "Schools are feeling lost when it comes to the world of social media. Teachers don't understand the online world and don't know how to be digital citizens themselves. Kids find it hard to engage with their teachers or parents, as their phones are their best friend and the online world is their safe space, where they can escape to. If you don't go and meet them in their space, they're reluctant to open up. Add social media platforms such as Instagram and TikTok into the mix and you see the dangers very clearly. Kids are doing things like creating confession pages on these apps, where you can anonymously paste anyone's photos or start vicious rumours. This is where a lot of mocking and bullying happens today – with deep effects and almost no repercussions. It's frightening," concludes Jorgensen.

There is also the myth that bullying ends when you leave school and tertiary education. One of the most lethal, toxic places can be the workplace, particularly in the corporate world, for any gender – although women are generally the targets here. Hearing stories ranging from being ignored at meetings, talked over and down to, to blatantly being blamed for others' wrongdoings, a corporate bully can have long-term effects on someone's work and emotional well-being.

Budding journalist Christal's* ambition of landing a job with a major magazine came true straight from college, and after a few years she was thrilled when what appeared to be her ideal job became a reality. But what started out as a dream ended in a real workplace nightmare. "For a 21-year-old girl from Mitchells Plain to suddenly find herself in this job was incredible to me. I was lucky because they could see I was naïve and inexperienced in the finer things in life, and for the next three years they went out of their way to nurture and encourage me, to the point where I was writing feature stories. When I was then offered a job as a features writer at another top magazine, I really thought my career had taken off. You can imagine my surprise when my new boss, instead of briefing me on my first feature, gave me a pile of papers to photocopy! I thought, oh well, I'm just starting so maybe I'm overreacting. But when she later pointed to a story by another feature writer and said, 'One day, you'll also get to write big features like that,' I felt truly insulted and should have seen that as the red flag it was. Right there and then, I should have confronted her as to why she hired me as a feature writer and was making such comments."

Types of bullies

Popular bullies

We've all met this type of bully – in both male and female forms. They're the ones with swagger, and egos to match. They're both confident and condescending, but somehow they usually come with groupies eager to be seen with the bully – whether as a schoolboy or an adult. Think Donald Trump and his entourage.

Another common trait is their sense of entitlement, which can grow alongside their power as a bully. Popular girls are more likely to use relational aggression (which I define below), spreading rumours, manipulating their peers and, of course, leaving certain girls out of their social realm.

You'll find popular bullies at the top of their game: maybe the school's star athlete or perceived school leader. In the workplace, unfortunately, they're often the boss; possibly middle management or even the CEO. As one woman commented to me when I asked her about her relationship with her "big boss", she replied that she'd rather get into trouble over something than ask him anything first. Her words were: "I'm terrified to go to him." Terrified is a strong word, and an awful weight to carry on a daily basis.

Three other women in the same department had suffered breakdowns, due to work pressure in a hostile environment. The amazing thing is, when you meet the boss he's the most charming man you could wish to encounter. This, of course, is on the surface – underneath there's the bully. Mention his name to anyone who knew him from school and you'll hear the same story – how he bullied them at school. Bullies rarely change. They like it at the top and do whatever it takes to stay there.

Relational bullies

Less obvious in style than most bullying, relational bullies don't necessarily fit the common bully stereotype but still carry a lot of influence. They are the ones who decide who's cool and who's not. They wield their power to exclude, isolate and ostracise anyone they feel deserves it. Their choice of weapon is verbal, not physical: spreading rumours, lies, gossip, labels and name calling, or worse, using emotional bullying to maintain control. This method is particularly favoured by "mean girls". Experts point out that this is because they're often jealous or feel they're socially unacceptable. As long as they're seen as the queen bee, they'll stop at almost nothing to keep that spot. Again, these bullies are not limited to schools, but are found in many workplaces.

It's not always easy to spot the relational bully, but be cautious if someone hurts other people's reputations, causes humiliation, encourages or rewards others to socially exclude another, and has no hesitation in publicly humiliating another person.

Serial bullies

The serial bully is often hard to pin down. This isn't an accident – they purposely keep a low profile although they're often one of the cool crowd, and as well as being strategic and controlled, they're completely calculated in their approach. Very few people have any idea what a serial bully is capable of.

One of the reasons why these bullies are difficult to recognise is that they'll suddenly appear just when you need a friend. You'll find them at school or in the workplace, generally hanging with a crowd, laughing and smiling and looking like someone you'd want to know. This is generally an act for an audience of teachers or their seniors. Once they befriend you, their true cold and calculating natures will gradually emerge.

Normal behaviour for the serial bully would be to abuse any authority they might have, inflict emotional blackmail, spread malicious gossip, and single you out when there's no one else around.

These bullies feature in this book, some as relationship partners who inflict pain, whether emotional or occasionally physical, on others their whole lives. The clever part is their skill at keeping their bullying under the radar and managing to maintain their innocence to such an extent that their victims feel powerless, as no one would ever believe them. In the business world this can have a bad ripple effect, not just on the careers of their colleagues but also on the business.

As long as you don't threaten the serial bully's job or popularity, you'll probably be safe, but cross that line and watch your back for your own job. They're exceptionally skilled at neutralising anyone that gets in their way. Once they get rid of someone, they'll sight their next target, and the next...

Sadly, the craving to feel recognised and needed often ends up seeing a serial bully being put in a position of power, which they'll then abuse.

Group bullies

Being picked on and bullied by an individual is bad enough, but when – particularly in a school setting – you're bullied by a group, things can turn nasty and dangerous very quickly. This is where pack mentality sets in, with one bully sparking off their group. These groups are often cliques that may have a leader members aspire to be like, even dressing similarly and copying their mannerisms. Being part of a group insulates individuals, making them far braver than they'd be on their own. If asked why they joined in the bullying, the answer is often simple: "Everyone else was doing it..."

Could YOU be a bully?

After reading this chapter, if you're worried you might be displaying some of the characteristics described, it's possible you may be a bully yourself. You could be a bully because someone is bullying you. If you are bullying, think about how it would make you feel if people were making fun of you, harassing you or stealing from you. It would make you feel awful, afraid and alone.

Are you bullying because it makes you feel powerful? Are you a kingpin because you are liked, or because people are scared of you? If this sounds familiar, you're probably already aware that what you are doing is wrong. If that is true, then take the first steps to altering your behaviour. Ask yourself:

- What made me start bullying?
- Why do I pick on people?
- How does it make me feel when I'm bullying somebody?

- If I want to, how do I stop?

If you're uncertain about what happens after you stop bullying, then speak to someone you trust not to judge you.

Adapted from Childline South Africa.[8]

CHAPTER 2

Bullying and teens

THERE ARE VERY few parents who aren't confronted with bullying at some point in their child's school years, either where their child is a bully, or is being bullied. As mentioned in the previous chapter, we have a visual image of the tough boy or girl as the bully and the bespectacled, timid child as the victim – but is this always the case?

Researchers have estimated that between 50 and 60 per cent of all South African school children are bullied in various forms, and although some kids are definitely more likely to be victims than others, bullying can happen to almost anyone, at any point in life – with the result often being psychological damage to last a lifetime.

In over 28 years of writing on mental health I've often encountered adults whose issues, when probed, will go back to that one touch point where they were bullied, incidents which left such an imprint on their psyches that they can generally recall every moment of those often vicious encounters.

According to clinical psychologist Liane Lurie, who has many years' experience working particularly with adolescents, "The teen years are exceptionally hard. With hormones raging, the academic and family demands and expectations placed on you, added to which you now have to cope with bullying, and you have a situation which is often completely out of your control."

A big part of any teenager's life today is social media and the digital world, which has further impacted the world of bullying, allowing cyberbullies to hide behind a computer and wreak havoc in others' lives.

"The digital world, particularly gaming, has added a whole new dimension to bullying," explains Cayley Jorgensen. "Whereas in the past with boys it was physical, as in pushing and shoving, today we're seeing far more bullying relating to gaming and the **side-texting** that goes on. It can be something as simple as someone makes mistakes, and doesn't hit the right keys at the right time, then someone else will quickly condemn them, asking, 'What's wrong with you?' or even threaten to do something ugly to their mother. This person is hiding behind a screen, so we don't know what their physical appearance is or how threatening they look in real life – but their words often hit home hard."

> **side-texting:** when you are engaged in an online interaction and one of the participants texts when they disagree with what is being said, or have additional information.

Why do kids bully?

As illustrated in the introduction, children can definitely start bullying before they can even walk. Although it's hard to picture a terrorising toddler everyone knows that children quickly learn the machinations of how to get their way, whether through beguiling smiles or literally throwing their toys out of the cot.

Lurie explains: "Unfortunately, when it does start at such a young age it can carry on throughout that person's life. There are many variables that come into play here: whether the child experienced abuse in their parents' marriage; how the trauma was dealt with by the family system; and what kind of discipline was there in the home. Were there inconsistent boundaries? How were emotions handled? Was there emotional validation, or did the child seek validation by bullying other children, and was there any impact from their actions?"

Whilst there are many explanations around why anyone becomes a bully, the dynamics are complex. According to Jorgensen, "What all bullies have in common is the power play. The types of online gaming bullies we talk about here, like all bullies, are looking to gain power, often trying to make themselves feel better. They think, 'I'll look cool if I'm nasty to these kids.'

"I believe that even a bully needs help. We need to lay down the consequences: 'What were you thinking?' They sometimes don't even realise or see that this is bullying. They'll tell you, 'I was only joking. I don't think I was being mean, I was just playing around.'"

So where do we draw the line between teasing and bullying? What is one person's teasing could well be another person's bullying. One of the tasks parents *should* undertake is to teach a child what bullying is and is not. This advice comes through as perhaps the strongest message in this book. If there's no one to teach that this type of behaviour is unacceptable and the toddler, child, teen or adult feels gratification doing it, then the cycle will continue.

"It all comes down to conversation and speaking openly because a lot of the time parents don't talk openly, especially about the online world. They might just take a device away as punishment, but generally the child will find it anyway," adds Jorgensen. "Often these kids are just copying what they see online, or they're feeling hurt, or they've been bullied themselves and are looking for revenge. I sometimes see bullies who are struggling academically, with their self-esteem taking a knock – there are so many different reasons here. Sometimes it's due to family problems at home or something happening in their community, or, of course, it could be that their parents are bullies themselves. Somehow they sense when someone has low self-esteem and will hone in on them. You'll often find that bullies who have been bullied see this as their way of paying it forward."

Jorgensen's observations are reinforced by Lurie. "We need to be courageous enough to have these conversations with our children, particularly where they may unintentionally be bullying by leaving someone out continuously. They don't see that as bullying, but of course it does irreparable harm to the child left out. We need to talk to them about the psychology of both the bully and the victim, what their roles are, and at the same time make it clear they need to come to you to openly discuss it without fear of being punished or getting into trouble, so that means of repair and healing can be put into place at both ends."

Perhaps, as is often the case, parents feel this is something the school will automatically teach, and the school feels is definitely the role of the parent. Maybe both should be teaching more about bullying – that way the messages would really hit home. Strangely enough, I found it particularly difficult to get parents to talk to me about bullying. I use the word strange, because there were plenty of children willing to speak but whose parents were more than a little reluctant to comment. Perhaps this is because it's difficult to admit your child has either been bullied or is a bully?

When it comes to understanding any form of child abuse, there is one expert's name that's a stand-out in this field and that's consultant Luke Lamprecht, who for three decades has been working in the non-profit and child protection sector, making a difference to each organisation he's involved in. Over this time he's "seen it all".

"Very often it's simply a case of parents being absent," explains Lamprecht. "When I grew up in the 1960s and 70s, we'd be involved with different groups of kids through sport or hobbies. This gave us a sense of belonging. Today when they're on their own, it's all about 'screen time'. They're left rudderless, without a sense of belonging. In the case of the kids I work with at Fight with Insight, a thriving inner-city community programme for children, using boxing to teach life skills, it's not about beating another person up, but quite the opposite. It's like martial arts, teaching kids to learn control and think before acting."

As we know, particularly in South Africa, many children grow up in homes where their parents are so busy trying to eke out a living that time with their children is at a premium.

"They're not being cruel – they just don't have a lot of time to spend with their kids. And other more advantaged parents are often too wrapped up in their own lives and their screens to even notice something is wrong.

"It's not always easy to pick up if a child is being bullied. If you're engaging with your child regularly you'll notice a change in their behaviour. They will suddenly go from being carefree to growing quiet, even aggressive, and snapping at you. This will often be put down to normal teen behaviour, which is where open communication is so important."

You will notice that this theme is a constant within these pages – open communication, which is something we all need to strive towards with our families. What is it that stops us from telling others when we're feeling hurt or abused?

Lamprecht is often called in to schools to advise on bullying issues. "It's always difficult when you have to talk to a parent. Being able to draw a line between real bullying and teasing is tricky. I try to empower the kids to be able to stand up for themselves without aggression. I try to teach them the power of being kind – no one really enjoys being horrible."

Reinforcing other expert opinions, Lamprecht emphasises the importance of really listening to your kids. "When a daughter comes home and says, 'Mom, this boy keeps looking at me funnily' and the mom replies, 'He must like you', that's not good enough, and doesn't help the child. Parents try to make excuses when they should be listening and trying to help arm their kids. When a kid suddenly doesn't want to go to school and you eventually get it out of them that they're being bullied, you need to ask the right questions. What kind of bullying is this? Tell me what happened. *Don't* ignore or minimise your child's being bullied. The long-term effects can be devastating," warns Lamprecht.

Girls and bullying

Mean girls – Jess's story

For Jess*, instead of the transition to high school seeing the bullying being left behind at primary school, it "infiltrated my life, carrying through to high school. One girl in particular would make you her 'best friend'. This entailed you not being allowed to be friends with anyone who could be more important than her. Like most bullies, she was very manipulative. When she saw that suddenly I was gaining confidence in something, or a boy liked me or something good was happening to me, she'd cry and say 'you've changed', making me feel terrible about myself. She had stopped me seeing all my other friends and they simply accepted that because she said so. She told one of my best friends that she wasn't allowed to go anywhere without her coming along. It took a while, but eventually I said I'm done with this friendship – I don't want this in my life.

"Having two older brothers and boy cousins, I could see that any bullying that went on with them was so different from girls. It didn't help that I went to a private all-girls school, with many girls coming from extremely wealthy and privileged backgrounds. My grandfather paid for my education so no one realised I was lower middle class." Jess's home life was already a difficult one, with her parents divorced and her mother going through her own crises.

"At first it was good just to have fun and not have to struggle with all the real-life stuff I was going through, but at the bottom of it I couldn't identify with the other girls. There were small things, such as if you wanted to be seen as cool you'd break the rule of your skirt having to touch your kneecaps. I couldn't identify with that, and after doing it for a while decided it just wasn't worth getting into trouble over. This and other things led to me becoming alienated from the cool crowd, particularly because I didn't want to disassociate myself from any one group of girls."

A situation that is perhaps as old as humanity itself is one person looking down on another: deeply entrenched superiority. Whether this is from a racial or cultural perspective, or from a class and financial status perspective – it's always been there and is likely to remain.

According to Lurie, "When you come from a less advantaged background into a school that's much more privileged and status-driven, you're often perceived as being far more vulnerable and insecure – that's when the bullies will prey on you. You've become a target for them. This is particularly relevant to girls, who often find it much harder to fit in, especially when material things like labels are used as a means of signifying status or a sense of belonging. In these types of situation these issues are far more amplified when it comes to bullying."

For Jess it wasn't so much about fitting in, but more about blending in without being in the limelight. She didn't seek to be part of a clique, which in a perverse way turned out to be difficult for her. "I took Zulu and so made friends with a lot of black girls in that group, and I'd often sit with them. The same with the music geeks – I was one of them. I became very close with some girls who were labelled nerdy – academics who were top of the class but not necessarily the prettiest. It was being friends with one such girl that saw the cool girls making my life hell. Going back to the skirt thing – I still remember the feeling of that skirt and feeling like a leper because I was seen as a nerd.

"I went to the headmistress, where I'd hoped to have an adult conversation to explain what was happening and that I was really struggling. I explained to her how these girls were spreading rumours about me and snickering behind their hands at me. The head's reaction: you don't talk about such things to the teachers! I was made to feel I was the problem and these were my issues. I wasn't supposed to make a scene. God forbid the image of the school should be tarnished.

"By the end of my first year there I wanted to leave, but my family persuaded me to give it one more term. So I returned the following year but nothing had changed – in fact it was worse, so I left and went to another private girls' school, but a much bigger one with a boys' school on the same campus. This somehow felt more normal to me, and I felt I had more chance of just blending in without drawing attention to myself."

For the next two years, school life was good for Jess and gradually she made different groups of friends. But things changed in Grade 10 when she started dating the coolest guy in matric. "Funnily enough, the things that were troubling the other girls were insignificant to me, compared to what I was struggling with at home. I couldn't relate to the gossip that went around and if you didn't take part in conversations around food and dieting, obsessively talking about weight, you were seen as thinking you were superior. It wasn't that at all – I just didn't get it...

"I remember a sudden shift and then I was being attacked. Suddenly I was getting picked on for different things I did, and when I defended myself it got worse. Now I was being phased out of my friendship groups and it was so difficult, I couldn't bear going to school. I'd have panic attacks at school and my dad would come and get me and bring me home. There wasn't much monitoring going on at home so I could get away with not going to school, but looking back I now realise I missed around half a term in my matric year. My home life at the time impacted me hugely. I grew up way too fast and although I was a teenager, I couldn't relate to teenage stuff. Not being the same as everyone else as an adult is celebrated, but at school this means automatic alienation.

"One of the girls told me some of the comments that were made to her, like 'Don't you find it really irritating when Jess laughs that way?' This planted a seed in my head and would worry me. My father's home tongue is Spanish, and at first when they'd hear me answer my phone, *'Hola, papi'*, they thought it was cute. She told me they had said this was stupid, and eventually she told me she couldn't stand being around me. Suddenly I was in the same situation I'd been in at my previous school."

I asked Jess if she talked to her parents about what was going on in her life. "My dad would point out that people who were mean like that were often dealing with their own stuff and that I shouldn't take it personally, which didn't really help. It didn't let up, it was a kind of subliminal brainwashing. I could literally feel the mood change when I walked into a room. Even though I'm now 31 this has carried through to this day, and I still worry that people find me annoying and that I have to apologise for being in their presence."

All this emotional bullying took its toll on Jess, leading to severe mental health challenges that are still ongoing. Therapy, although at times hard, is essential to her well-being. "The sessions are sometimes difficult and I have to push myself but I feel so heard and understood, which really takes so much weight off me. There's no blueprint on how to run your life – it's about different perspectives from people who have your best interests at heart. My therapist has shown me that although it's true that I feel I annoy people with my presence, at the same time it's not reality.

"I just want people to know that bullying becomes very deep-rooted.

Two of the girls who were my nemeses have reached out to me in the last couple of years to 'make things right', but I decided they have no place in my life. They were incredibly toxic and there are enough people in the world for me to connect with, and have positive relationships. Now I get to choose who I want to spend time with and can avoid toxic people, who are easy to spot. I don't have to see my friends all the time and sometimes might not speak to them for months, but I know we add value to each other's lives. That should be the motive for friendship. I look for kindness now. If you're kind, everything else follows."

A lesson I've learnt whilst researching this book is that although the end results of ongoing torment are generally the same, there is no one route on this journey. Bullying can affect anyone, from any type of background, at any time. People I've known for years who on the outside seem fine were, when I mentioned I was writing this book, quick to flash back on memories of their bullying experiences and how it made them feel – and in some cases how it had impacted their confidence levels going forward in life.

Back to school – Caitlyn's story

Twenty-three-year-old Caitlyn's[*] story is different to Jess's in that her home life was stable, with both parents fully involved in her life. But for Caitlyn that became a problem. "When the bullying started in prep school, the last thing I wanted was my parents involved. The main bully's mom was a teacher and each time an incident happened she'd team up with her daughter to support her, while saying at the same time, 'I'm not taking my daughter's side...' But of course she did. I felt if I told my parents and they came to the school, my life would have been even more miserable."

Caitlyn's problems had started in prep school when she suddenly started putting on weight, which other kids were quick to point out in a negative way. By the time she reached high school she was acutely aware of her shape. "I loved swimming and had previously swum for my school before injuring my shoulder. When I felt I wanted to return to the pool I asked the same bully from prep school, who was also a swimmer, how the swimming was at this school. Her answer: 'You're going to put *that* body into a swimming costume?'" After this, covering her body up as much as she could was Caitlyn's answer. "I always felt people were looking at me and by the end of Grade 8 I left the school and went to boarding school in KwaZulu-Natal. Why I thought this would be better I'm not sure, as once again the girls were cliquey and bullying was rife."

She managed to make some like-minded friends, but being an elite girls' boarding school, she was again faced with the same type of situation. "'If you don't have the money, you're not part of us', was made evident at this school," she explains.

"One of the girls I'd become friends with had a boyfriend at our brother school, half an hour away. I'd known him since we were children and we'd always been friends. Everything was fine until he broke up with her, and she started spreading rumours that I'd slept with him. Suddenly the word was out – I was a slut. This was one of the hardest things I'd ever had to deal with, particularly as I'd been raped the year before." To escape the hurt and pain Caitlyn started to cut herself, which she says was her way of stopping herself taking her own life.

"My parents were aware of my unhappiness and after I lost a best friend that year, I started seeing a psychologist. But no one knew about the rape – until recently. The worst part of being accused of sleeping with this other girl's boyfriend was that girls I thought were my good friends actually believed it. What I realised later was that the girl who had been ditched was the popular girl, and it was either be on her good side or you were out. I wanted to leave the school but was persuaded to stay with promises being made to me by the principal about what they were going to do about bullying. Promises that were never kept. This meant that for the next year, every time I would see a group of girls in a huddle whispering, I thought it was about me. My anxiety levels were sky-high and I was diagnosed with narcolepsy. I knew I just had to keep my head down and finish the matric year."

The bullying even influenced Caitlyn's decision on where to go to university – anywhere the bully and her gang were not applying to. After starting university and changing course after a year, she finally found what she really wanted to study, which was going well until Covid changed everything. "For me it was great, as it gave me the opportunity to be on my own. I also saw a new therapist and a psychiatrist as I was in a bad place. They both helped me so much; they made one hundred per cent difference to my life. Without them, I don't know that I'd still be here.

"Over the years I've lost many friends to suicide, and that's why I want to speak out about bullying. If someone is being ugly to you, you shouldn't take it, because if you take it once it's going to happen over and over again. Words get embedded in the back of your mind and you'll hear them over and over again."

Whilst she's not quite out of the woods yet, Caitlyn has come a long way in the last couple of years. "I'm getting there – taking my power back. I used to let people walk all over me. Today, I can stand up for myself. I'm never going to let this happen to me again."

When I hear stories like Caitlyn's, I can't help but think that perhaps what schools should be looking to incorporate into general learning is self-confidence, mixed with a healthy dose of self-worth and self-esteem. I had parents who provided this for me, with my father in particular always telling me that no one was better than me and that I must never let anyone, man or woman, intimidate me just because they are in a position of power, for instance. This has stood me in good stead over the years, particularly when it comes to interviewing high-powered business people and even presidents.

What happened to Caitlyn though, according to Vanessa Richards, a clinical social worker, is often the norm these days, particularly in all-girls schools. "**Cancel culture**, where someone is ostracised, reigns supreme today, with teenage girls being particularly good at it. Girls are socialised to bully at a relational level, with some of the ways they do it being slut shaming, spreading rumours and unfollowing friends on social media. Boys are still socialised around a particular version of masculinity that's about power and aggression."

> **cancel culture:** a way of behaving in a society or group, especially on social media, in which it is common to completely reject and stop supporting someone because they have said or done something that offends you; also known as "call out culture".

Boys will be boys...

High school horror – Grant's story

What does the phrase "boys will be boys" actually mean? That it's okay to excuse violent behaviour from men and boys because this is part of their "essential character"? That it's okay to kick another boy's legs out from under him when he's on the sports field, or push him into the wall as you walk by? For 21-year-old Grant*, this was his everyday high school experience – one he definitely didn't want to share with his parents for fear of being called a mommy's boy. "This was the worst thing you could do. If you show any form of weakness to bullies they use it as bait. Although I knew my mom would always listen and try and give me good advice, my parents had no idea of the extent of what I went through.

"At high school the jocks are the heroes and somehow they also seem to head up the bullies. I quickly learnt to stay off social media, which would just intensify the bullying." But the bullying eventually led to Grant being diagnosed with anxiety and depression, which he'd still downplay so as not to get his parents involved.

Just like in the animal world, where it's said that animals can sense fear and weakness, bullies also feed off shyness and timidity. For Grant, showing any sign of weakness would immediately attract the bullies' attention: "By the time I got beyond Grade 8, things became very scary for me.

"The school's attitude was, let's throw a little counselling into classes, but of course everyone just sat there – no one put their hands up and spoke about what was going on. Did I want to say what they threatened to do sexually to my mom? Of course I did, but I knew this would fall on deaf ears and nothing would change, except I'd be bullied even more. I'd had first-hand experience of this when we were learning about the reproductive system and a boy brought porn to school. I reported it and something was done about it, but from then on I was known as 'the snitch'."

Now at university and doing well, Grant can look back on his time at school and talk dispassionately about it. "I was always comparing myself to others, which wasn't healthy at all and contributed a lot to my mental health issues. I now know I have to take what I have, and make my own story and my own life. I feel as though I'm definitely taking huge steps and feel a lot more confident in myself.

"My parents, when they found out exactly what I'd gone through at high school, felt really bad that they hadn't done enough." A common situation, but perhaps a catch-22, with parents' involvement leading to more bullying.

Gender, sexual orientation and your teen

"It will be much easier, over time, to change attitudes towards race than it would be to alter beliefs about sexuality."
– Professor Jonathan Jansen, Distinguished Professor of Education, Stellenbosch University

It's tough enough being a teen without the added complications of coming out to friends and family as gay, **transgender** or **non-binary**.

Throw any of these identities into a culture where they are not easily accepted and you have twice the problems and anxiety most kids could possibly handle. Sadly, this is an area that most parents and teachers will avoid discussing.

> **transgender or trans:** an umbrella term to refer to people whose gender identity and/or gender expression differ(s) from the sex assigned to them at birth. **non-binary:** a gender identity that does not conform to traditional binary beliefs about gender, which indicate that all individuals are exclusively either male or female.

Growing up knowing people with different sexual orientations and with parents who taught me to accept everyone's lifestyle has made a huge difference to my own levels of acceptance and understanding as an adult. But this certainly isn't the norm, as I quickly discovered during my research.

Acceptance in Alex – Thabo's story

Sixteen-year-old Thabo* lives in Alexandra township in Johannesburg. A poverty-stricken urban neighbourhood, Alex can be a tough place to grow up – where any gender or sexual orientation difference generally involves hiding your true self from others. In rural schools being LGBTQIA+ is linked to being possessed by "evil spirits", with very little, if any, education around these issues being given. And in townships the situation is pretty similar. This obviously isn't just confined to African culture, with many other cultures being equally dismissive of any way of being that doesn't fit into an accepted version of gender and social "normality". When talking to a group of students from the Alexandra Education Committee, I heard this very touching story, made even more moving by the support of his peers.

"Since coming out to my family last year I've been bullied a lot," explains soft-spoken, shy Thabo. "It's meant being excluded from certain things, and even my own brothers have rejected me at times because of me expressing who I am openly. It's really put me through a lot and I've suffered from anxiety and depression as a result. A lot of people may look at me and see this happy soul, but I'm just hiding the pain with a smile. My advice to other people going through this is to stay strong and have faith. Somewhere along the way they'll all accept you for what you are.

"Luckily my mom has friends in the LGBT community and things are fine with her, but with my brothers it's still hectic, which means I can't express myself freely within my house."

As I stood listening to Thabo tell me his story, another young man wanted to add his comments and, addressing Thabo directly, said, "You must say, 'This is who I am, accept me for this'. Thabo, be yourself. Talk to people who support you and accept you for what you are. Don't change for others. Don't let negative thoughts get into your head. People are always going to judge you on everything you do. Just be you." I felt so good hearing these comments, and found myself hoping that Thabo took these words on board.

The "different" child

Whether a child has a physical or mental disability, they are seen as being different to other kids. For these children and their parents, this is a difficult path to navigate.

"Otherness" is how Vanessa Richards describes this category of bullying. "This, together with intolerance and a culture of moral disengagement, is when bullies feel it's almost legitimate for certain people to be targeted. Anyone who is seen as 'other' in their eyes is fair game. The more rigid and structured the environment is, such as a traditional old school, the more that person's otherness is made visible."

Ilana Gerschlowitz, a mother of three boys (two of whom were diagnosed with autism) and founder and director of The Star Academy, is no stranger to bullying. I'd worked with Ilana on her book *Saving My Sons: A Journey with Autism* and witnessed first-hand how, even though she'd lived with the realities of bullying for many years, she was deeply aware of the hurt involved.

"It's not so much the profoundly autistic children who face bullying, but autism being a spectrum sees higher functioning kids more likely to be bullied. These children have got a social-skills deficit, so they're not going to pick up social cues so easily. They're not going to be adept at joining a conversation or perhaps at being interested in the same things as their peers. They may be a bit quirky, and self-esteem is often an issue when it comes to autism," says Gerschlowitz.

"We frequently have higher functioning autistic kids at school who are being bullied, and one of the first things we do is to determine which developmental skills they're missing so we can teach them those social skills – so they won't be a sitting duck to a bully. We'll often focus on assertiveness; that if you're being bullied, go and tell someone in authority. We talk them through different ways they can be assertive. The second thing is building their self-esteem and getting them to understand that they may be good at certain things, but not so much at other things. Then we look at how to balance this out and improve the areas they lack in, particularly social skills, so they can make friends."

For Rebecca van Wyngaard, one of Ilana's teachers at The Star Academy, all of whom are qualified in ABA (Applied Behaviour Analysis), bullying – particularly with high school learners on the autism spectrum – is not something new. "Because the learners don't always appear as though they know what's going on around them, this leads to peers and even teachers talking about them directly in front of them – thinking they won't understand the comments passed, which are often deeply hurtful.

"Kids on the spectrum battle to pick up on sarcasm or understand humour, which again makes life difficult for them, especially when they're interacting with their peers. The funny thing is, these kids are often seen as wanting to be by themselves, when in fact they often seek out companionship, which without social skills means making friends is a tall order."

Whilst the need is there to make friends, it's often difficult for those on the spectrum to regulate their emotions, which can sometimes be read as aggressive or socially unacceptable, scaring off any possible friends. "As they get older, these kids become more self-aware and recognise the difference between themselves and other kids. This in turn leads to low self-esteem, anxiety and depression, even to self-harm and suicidal ideation.

"It's up to parents of any child who's 'different' to be their child's advocate," explains Rebecca. "Schools are often unaware that bullying is even happening, so the parent has to report it. What would be great is if schools who have children with any differences such as autism could educate the other learners, maybe through videos or guest speakers, just what these children are going through. It's important to create a safe space where they feel heard and no one is going to judge them. It would be great if there was a way of linking them with a buddy or preferred teacher at school to help them when there are no other adults they trust. As they get older, we're able to teach them more assertiveness skills," she concludes.

Warning signs of physical or verbal bullying from SADAG:

- Unexplainable injuries.
- Lost or destroyed clothing, books, electronics or jewellery.
- Social withdrawal, such as sudden loss of friends or avoidance of social situations.
- Refusal to say what's wrong.
- Frequent headaches or stomach aches, feeling sick or feigning illness, and making excuses not to go to school.
- Changes in eating habits, like suddenly skipping meals or binge eating. Kids may come home from school hungry because they didn't get to eat their own lunch.
- Difficulty sleeping or frequent nightmares.
- Declining academic performance and loss of interest in schoolwork.
- Feelings of helplessness or decreased self-esteem.
- Self-destructive behaviours such as running away from home, self-harm or talking about suicide.

Helping your child – the bully

Sometimes this is as easy as parents taking a cold, hard look at themselves. Are your children simply mimicking what they see at home? I remember only too clearly the first time one of my kids suddenly dropped the "f" bomb – in front of my horrified mother! I rushed to assure her they hadn't heard this at home, but I guess it most certainly could have been. "This doesn't mean you're teaching your child to swear – it's that the child is modelling your behaviour," explains Cayley Jorgensen. "Very often when we tell a parent their child is bullying, their reaction is, 'No, that's impossible, it must be someone else.' Slow down there. If your child is the bully we can handle it, but the most important thing to understand is that they need help. What do you as a parent need to do?

"This is where life lessons come in, and explaining just what is and isn't bullying. It's about open conversation with your kids. It's not the end of the world, but [the behaviours] can't be overlooked. Face up to the fact that your child is a bully, and think about what they're going to be like by the time they're in the workplace," says Jorgensen.

Let's face it – parenting is hard. Kids don't come with a manual, but being "prepared to parent" is a big issue these days. I remember only too well the pain of teaching my then toddlers the importance of sharing their toys – no small child really wants to do this and as a new parent you don't have built-in skills to teach this. I had an advantage in that I worked from home in those days, so it was easier for me to step in and engage in moments of conflict than other parents who aren't always there to teach their children these vital lessons. A nursery school teacher with a full class can't be expected to have her eyes everywhere. And there are certainly more issues to deal with these days than when I was a new mother.

"There are so many stressors around right now," says Liane Lurie. "Financial pressures and general stresses of life are quite different today. Things have changed, with families becoming far more fragmented. Many families who have emigrated, for instance, find themselves without the same type of support system they had. Add to this the recent Covid outbreak that saw parents and kids all at home, and things are pretty tough out there.

"The other scenario we see often is parenting in absentia, using au pairs and nannies to take care of parenting. This means kids only see their parents at night and on weekends, so when they do have access to their parents they feel negative attention is better than no attention."

Being present for your children, even when you're not in the same room as them, comes up in the stories of many people on both ends of the bullying spectrum.

Helping your child – who's being bullied

On the other side of the coin, if your child is being bullied they also need to feel safe speaking up. I asked former headmaster and educationalist Paul Channon, who has seen many children and parents pass through his doors over the years, how one empowers your child? "I think a lot has to do with just how well you know your child. It's often about being able to judge where your child is, emotionally. Today, so many parents put huge emphasis on academics over and above what's really going on with their child.

"Working with children from townships in our Alexandra Education Committee, we see these expectations multiplied a hundredfold. They are honourable motives, with parents who had a life of misery wanting their child to have more opportunities – but this comes with massive pressure on the child to be able to change the parents' lives. I've had boys weeping in my office who are often battling at varsity but can't tell their parents. It's all about expectations and marks. These are different forms of bullying – family bullying being one. We generally find complex kids come from complex family situations. But all parents must be careful what they lay on their child – these high expectations often land up with the child suffering from depression and anxiety, amongst other things.

"In previous generations, and even now, one of the most common things a parent would say is 'Hit them back', but is this the way to go? Most research on this issue shows conclusively the answer is no! Generally, I've found this just makes the situation worse, especially if the bully is the bigger of the two. One parent said to me that yes, they did tell their child to hit back because they didn't want their kid to be seen as someone who could be pushed around. For so long this kind of violence has been seen as part of being a boy or a man – part of their masculinity. But does this still apply today – do we not need our sons to grow up being more sensitive to other people's feelings without being labelled as a sissy?"

Lurie's plea is that kids need to feel free to talk to their parents and teachers about what's happening to them. "They need to be able to tell someone they trust, and be able to tell them just what they want them to do. This is a big responsibility – to intervene and make sure it doesn't happen again.

"Many kids are scared to speak up. They're afraid of not being believed or that they'll be blamed for making the bullying happen. And on the school side they're afraid of being called a snitch or mummy's pet, worsening the whole situation. But the consequences of doing nothing are far worse. If you're afraid of being bullied, or you're being bullied, then make sure you're never alone with the bully. That's when a bully feels the strongest – when there's no one else to witness their actions."

As a parent myself, I understand that the most normal reaction when you hear your child has been bullied is to want to take action quickly and confront the bully, and often the school, on what's been happening. According to Jorgensen, this isn't the best course of action. "Parents often react before they really listen or respond to what their child is telling them. Many times, kids will pretend everything is fine because they're scared of the reaction they'll get. What they need most is to be heard and to open up about what they're feeling. In such an emotionally charged situation, that fear of how everyone else is going to react is enough to stop the truth emerging.

"It's never too early to start building this type of trust between parents and kids. As soon as a child can understand, that's when open conversations need to start. It's also important for parents to know the signs. How do you know your child is the victim, how to notice changes in their behaviour. As they grow and develop, carry on having these open conversations at their level, not just from an adult's perspective. Most important is to really listen before offering advice – allow them to be really heard, commenting, 'I completely understand; this must be so difficult for you; I hear what you're saying.' By trying to understand what they saw and felt, you're connecting rather than correcting."

One thing's for sure: when you get an inkling that something isn't right with your teen, don't brush it off or tell them to "tough it out". Every person deserves a sense of safety and self-worth and if you do nothing this could lead, as it has in many cases, to suicide.

Some tips for parents from Luke Lamprecht:

- Stay calm when you're listening to the issue.
- Familiarise yourself with the facts about bullying and the forms it takes (to understand the difference between bullying and normal peer conflict).
- Ask your child what they have already done to stop the bullying.
- Discuss ways of deflecting the bully's unwanted attention.
- Help your child keep a record of when, where and how the bullying took place, and who was involved.
- If the bullying continues, arrange a meeting with the school.
- Encourage your child to talk about it and hand over the record.
- Allow time for the school to investigate, but arrange a date for a progress report.
- Keep talking until the bullying stops.
- Encourage your child to have a buddy.

CHAPTER 3

Bullying and the role of schools

SO, WHERE SHOULD schools step in when it comes to bullying, and how far should they go in terms of both educating their pupils around bullying and at the same time meting out punishment to the bullies? Quite a number of people I spoke to felt schools are too reluctant to get involved, and could spend more time educating learners on topics relating to bullying and the importance of understanding and kindness.

As I've mentioned, I initially approached quite a number of schools to get their input for this book and also to gain permission to speak to their pupils. I hit a complete wall, and I have to say I was shocked that not only did I not get any replies but I didn't even receive any acknowledgement of my requests, bar one school.

This isn't the first time this has happened to me, as over the years when I've worked on stories about drugs in schools and other investigative pieces involving high school or primary school learners I've had many doors closed in my face. These were requests around issues I *knew* were happening, and I just wanted to give schools the opportunity to discuss them with me and talk about how they were handling matters. Instead, I found school administrators would rather just pretend these were topics that didn't affect them and carry on as normal. Except for the fact that bullying, as with drugs and other issues, does happen on a daily basis in schools, and wishing the problem away isn't going to make it go away.

There have been a number of acts related to bullying passed over the years in South Africa, but these have to be embraced and put into action by individual schools. The question must be asked – are they doing this? Bullying hasn't been recognised as a specific crime in South

Africa yet, but the law does safeguard children's rights to dignity and safety. Two stand-out laws protect children's constitutional rights.

The South African Schools Act 84 of 1996:

- Contains specific clauses regarding the rights of learners, which include non-discrimination and equality; privacy, respect and dignity; and non-violence, freedom and security.
- Specifies that victimisation, bullying and intimidation of other learners are offences that may lead to suspension.
- Requires school governing bodies to adopt a code of conduct for learners, which the school must enforce.
- Deals specifically with the prohibition of initiation practices (in Section 10 A), and explicitly prohibits endangerment of mental or physical health or safety, undermining of human dignity, humiliating or violent acts, and destruction of private property.

The Children's Act 38 of 2005:

- Emphasises protecting children against abuse and neglect.
- Specifically includes bullying by another child as an offence in its definition of abuse – the only act to do this.
- Makes provision (in Section 14) for the child's right to bring or be assisted to bring a matter to court, including bullying.

As someone who has many years' experience in the field, former headmaster Paul Channon firmly believes that every school leader faces the problem of bullying and how to stop it, if you ever can. "The problem is, there are stories and there are perceptions. For example, a child claims they have been bullied because another child looked at them strangely. Typically a parent will take their child's side, even if there's little evidence to back up whether the child's perception of the incident is accurate. So much depends on the psyche of the child and their perception of the situation. On the other side, the school needs to know what is actually going on.

"If you question the child who is accused, they'll say, 'I was just going to the loo – I don't remember looking at him strangely.' The other child was perhaps quite timid, which created this situation. Now parents on both sides are defensive or angry, with the school caught in the middle. You can't take sides as you weren't there, so how do you deal with a situation like this? Depending on the openness of the parents, you can try and get them all to come in to sort things out. But if they come bringing their own issues, the situation can become inflamed.

"Having come from a background of working in boys' schools, there are now terms such as 'toxic masculinity' that weren't there before. High schools today are generally more aware of creating the right culture. And of course, the impact of social media has made a massive difference."

> **toxic masculinity:** a set of attitudes and ways of behaving stereotypically associated with or expected of men, regarded as having a negative impact on men and on society as a whole.

One of the hot topics involving bullying over the last few years, particularly at boys' high schools, has been around initiation rites, often with major media headlines as a result. For some past pupils their initiation will bring back memories of bonding and fun, but for very many others I've spoken to over the years it's their worst memory of school. Today, schools promise these "barbaric" rituals will stop, but do they?

"The headmaster of a leading boys' school recently took on this type of culture, and it certainly wasn't welcomed by the senior boys," explains Channon. "What he did was to make each matric boy take on a new boy coming into the school in the role of a mentor, and make sure the younger boy wasn't being bullied and that his transition to high school was smooth. The senior boys saw this as the headmaster taking away their privileges and their power. Such a decision isn't easy for the head of a school. You need to be made of stern stuff to take on such an established culture. Most see it as easier to ride the waves, putting out fires as they come up.

"Some kids thrive on this culture – others not. I've met people who, simply from attending a school camp, have been damaged for life. It's often hard for kids not to be picked on. It's all about the group dynamic, the culture of the school and the child's psyche. When you bring the three together, it can either lead to growth or a damaging experience. What this means is that you have to try and find the right fit for your child – if this is possible. When you're in a non-changing dynamic, you have five years of misery which can damage your entire life. Kids don't always speak to their parents about things and they're often too young to process what's happening. For them, it would just confirm their inadequacy. In their internal world it teaches them they're hopeless: 'No one wants to be my friend'. They may find themselves in a group of outliers – not really where you want to be in high school. And we haven't mentioned girls, who are generally worse when it comes to doing damage through bullying," concludes Channon.

Choosing a school for your child isn't always easy, as where you live generally dictates your options. It's not easy to judge the right fit for a child at primary school, but by the time it comes to finding a high school for your child, if you have a choice then try your best to match the school to your child. Don't send them to a school renowned for its academic prowess if they're not academic, and the same goes for sport.

When one of my own children was in Grade 2, I attended a soccer game where the parents ran up and down the sidelines yelling instructions at their offspring. No one told them to stop and it was apparent that this was a school where winning at all costs was important. I had my son's name down for the senior phase of this school and, even though he was only seven at the time, I called the school and asked them to remove his name from their list. I didn't want my son to grow up with this type of ethos. I didn't want him to have to worry that every time he made a wrong move on the field he would have the whole team, coaches and parents coming down on him.

It's not a case of teaching your child to accept losing as the norm, but to understand that winning a school sport's game isn't what frames you as a person for life.

Cowboys don't cry

"It's important to show a boy that you can still be a man, show emotion and cry – that it's okay," explains Liane Lurie. "One school I went to had rugby initiation every year, where the matrics got into a lot of trouble, often losing their prefect status. The school came down so hard on them, although the sports coaches and managers of the teams, who knew full well about this tradition, never suffered a single consequence. It's difficult for schools, but something has to change."

"When a kid is told to 'toughen up – be a man', it invalidates the extent of the trauma and the impact it had on them, in what they experienced. Teaching kids 'an eye for an eye' and that you must bully as a response is counter-productive, but showing them there are other avenues and other outcomes that are possible, and that as an adult you're prepared to step in to protect them and speak on their behalf, is validating. Generally this is not what the child wants, but what this does do is contribute to a sense of self-isolation, with the teen feeling like a failure. I can't defend myself and in the eyes of my parents, who I want the most validation from, I'm a wuss. I'm less than…

"So much depends on the school system you're working with. At a school with multi-level interventions, involving all stakeholders including learners, parents, teachers, school governing bodies, then they may be more receptive to your coming forward. It also depends on the kind of school and upbringing the parent or child comes from.

Very often, parents live vicariously through their kids and they see the bullying as a comment on themselves – and they refuse to make themselves vulnerable enough to see that they can be part of the solution."

At the same time schools are also worried about their reputation, explains Lurie. "Very often learners and parents will question a school's reaction to bullying as, 'Is it coming from a place of caring, or do they care more about reputational damage?' What is needed from schools is a change of attitude. This obviously doesn't apply to all schools, as today there's much more awareness. But at the same time there are real legal implications. Parents can file for protection from harassment, for instance, which can make a school feel vulnerable."

At FaceUp South Africa, they've seen a change in attitudes in the last four years. "We've found there is the space to talk up. The minute you say to learners there is help for you if you can speak up, without fear of reprisals, there's a huge change and shift in terms of feeling the teachers care. It's so important that learners understand they can speak up without getting into trouble for it," emphasises FaceUp director Cayley Jorgensen.

So what are the factors that need to be looked at when it comes to change in schools around bullying?

- What kind of reporting climate does the school have?
- How effective are teacher responses to reports of bullying?
- Are there strong student-teacher relationships?
- Are teachers supported?
- Is there engagement in social activities where education around bullying would be involved?

Jorgensen explains that getting schools to buy in to their FaceUp programmes, even though they know they have bullying problems, isn't always easy. "Many schools will tell you they don't have bullying, but when we offer to give them a free pilot trial, they'll generally agree."

Although, points out social worker Vanessa Richards, despite the fact there are various laws and human rights protections in place, with schools issuing government-designed anti-bullying policies, the success rate of these isn't high, particularly when it comes to teaching youngsters how not to be victims. "I see it as the bureaucracy of bullying and interpersonal violence. There's a policy with multi-level reporting procedures, which categorises bullying into certain contexts. What it doesn't allow for are the types of bullying which fall outside these guidelines. Add to this tired, burnt out and overburdened teachers who would rather look the other way than wade through a mountain of paperwork. What happens when these incidents go from bullying to violence is that teachers don't know how to deal with or classify this."

Even though not all schools are equal in terms of facilities and staff in South African society, I found that how bullying is handled has nothing to do with resources and everything to do with the heads of the schools and the staff themselves.

Lurie firmly agrees when it comes to the inefficacy of anti-bullying policies: "Unless there is systemic involvement and buy in from the whole school community, including parents, it can't work."

When schools get serious about bullying

The renowned and highly successful Westerford High School not only take this subject seriously, but allowed me to sit down with a group of their learners.

When I arrived at the school, my first impressions were of the openness and friendliness of the teachers and the respect the pupils showed both to them and me as a visitor. Teaching these young adults the importance of respect has certainly paid off. Deputy Principal Alison Gray, with 20 years' experience in various teaching roles at the school, was only too happy to share their experiences with me.

"So much has changed during this time, particularly in the last two to three years with the growth of social media. We often know who's making hurtful remarks, while they think their screens protect their identity. Even the way kids speak to one another has changed with phrases like, 'You're a retard', 'That's so stupid', and 'That's so gay' becoming almost normalised between them. When they're hiding behind a screen, they seem to gain more courage to be even more hurtful. I like to think we don't have a tremendous amount of bullying at our school, but one of our biggest problems when it comes to bullying is definitely social media.

"We like to say that we're not a progressive school but a progressing school. We tend to be half a step in front of a lot of other traditional schools. We developed two policies. One is an anti-racism policy statement, which is essential in a school like ours with such huge diversity in both the student body and staff. This also encompasses an inclusivity policy, meaning that where a pupil, teacher or ground staff member feels their human rights have been infringed, they can take it not just to one person but to an independent committee made up of a group of diverse people who will deal with it."

In the last few years there have been quite a number of debates in schools (generating media headlines) around learners' rights related to hair, jewellery and clothing policies, often linked to gender, culture and race. I asked Gray how they dealt with these issues. "For the most part we've kept clear of these issues. A good few years ago we changed our hair and jewellery policy for both boys and girls. At first we were criticised for letting boys grow their hair and wear earrings, for instance, but when people saw that they still looked neat and well-presented it became a non-issue."

Restorative justice

Agreeing with other educationalists interviewed for this book, Gray talks about how difficult it is to deal with "he said, she said" accusations. "We've had some sexual assault claims over the years which have been very much like that, and it's a very fine line to walk. Even if you believe the boy more than the girl, how do you say to the girl, 'We don't believe you'? We try to look at **restorative justice** rather than look for a punishment. If it becomes a complete stalemate then we have to say this was perceived as bullying, therefore you must go on this particular course. We then talk to whichever counsellor they see to resolve issues. But finding out who's guilty and who the victim is, is often really difficult.

> **restorative justice:** process in which the aim is not to punish a bully but to rehabilitate, by restoring the imbalance between bully and victim through specific programmes.

"When there's a clear case of ongoing bullying which can be proved, this would then be escalated to a disciplinary hearing. But even if we do recommend something like expulsion, because we're a government school this would have to be ratified by the Department of Basic Education, which makes this a major issue. This is another reason for trying restorative justice before taking disciplinary action.

"We've had incidents with Grade 8s, where stupid comments have been made here and there and then a phone call will be made to their parents to explain what happened and how we're going to deal with it. We ask the parents to also talk to their child at home, as we feel bringing in parents fairly early in this process generally helps. Parents need to be kept in the loop, as very often the cause of the hurtful comments comes from the home."

By the time I started wrapping up research for this book, I realised that Westerford's way of dealing with such issues is very definitely in the minority.

When playground bullying goes viral

Not all bullying involves just words. When it leads to violence, it leaves the realm of bullying and becomes assault and a criminal act. One such incidence of violence was in April 2021, when a Grade 10 Limpopo schoolgirl took her own life by overdosing on pills, after being violently beaten by a fellow pupil at her high school.

Perhaps the worst part was the group of other girls who gathered around the fight with their phones, cheering on the two girls whilst filming the incident, which then saw the video clip go viral on social media. When this happens it's not always to highlight the sheer horror of the scenario but just as much for the voyeuristic value! By simply standing, watching or even cheering the bully on, makes that bystander just as much a bully.

The shame of this incident was simply too much for this young girl, and as soon as she reached home she locked herself in her room and swallowed the pills that would take her life.

The MEC for Education in Limpopo at the time, Polly Boshielo, quickly issued a statement condemning such conduct that had turned the province's schools into horrendous havens of those who have no regard for their peers. "Bullying is wrong and will never be tolerated in our schools," she said.[9] Boshielo also promised that those involved would "face the music".

The 14-year-old perpetrator, who was arrested for this incident, was released to her mother's care on R1 500 bail after spending a few weeks in a place of safety. According to her mother, she was "remorseful" on how this incident played out and will have to live with the guilt. The point is, of course, how do we change these behaviours?

In the past the cry might have been something like, "But kids are exposed to this type of violence on television all the time – it must rub off on them." Today, it's not just television promoting these behaviours but other media, particularly gaming. But is that enough to cause this behaviour?

"Generally with groups of girls it depends on the group dynamic and very often a ring leader, who's the popular and powerful cool girl the other girls are very scared to stand up to," explains Lurie. "If they do stand up to her or voice their disagreement, they'll likely be kicked out of the group, and for adolescents social suicide is one of the worst crimes. Fitting in is so important, so they go along with whatever's happening. They may feel they're bystanders and powerless, but they're actually complicit in allowing the bullying to happen."

Jorgensen adds, "With this terrible incident in Limpopo, she was physically bullied with those standing around recording it. So what does that make the kids recording it? Half the kids would say they're the bullies, with the other half saying, no, they're trying to create awareness of the bullying!"

The Bullying Circle

Starts the bullying and takes an active part

Bully

Takes an active part, but does not start the bullying — **Bully**

Dislikes the bullying and helps or tries to help the victim — **Hero**

Supports the bullying, but does not take an active part — **Bully**

Victim

Dislikes the bullying and thinks he/she should help, but does not — **Bully**

Likes the bullying, but does not display open support — **Bully**

Watches what happens but does not take a stand — **Bully**

Graphic adapted from The Olweus Bullying Prevention Group.[10]

"This isn't just a phenomenon in any one type of school," explains Lurie. "Physical bullying amongst girls exists across all environments. It can be a learnt behaviour or simply that girls feel they don't have the means to express anger, disapproval or aggression in more conventional, stereotypical ways through dialogue. So they look at what the ultimate way is to shame someone or inflict both verbal and physical punishment on them. Very often, the person being bullied will have lost trust in the system and even though they have reported things before, they weren't taken seriously or it's been reduced to normal teen behaviour. They might also feel they can't report incidents because the consequences will be worse, or that their parents are under so much strain and stress in other areas they can't add an additional burden. Worst scenario, they actually believe they deserve this abuse."

Not wanting to add to their parents' burden was a common theme when I spoke to young people, particularly during Covid: "My parents already have so much to deal with..." The problem for parents, though, is when something really bad then happens, they're the ones saying, "If only I'd known..."

Law and order

Through Paul Channon I was able to talk to a large group of the kids he works with from the Alexandra Education Committee, all from different schools, and they were open about the issues they were facing as young students coming from underprivileged backgrounds.

When I asked for teens to volunteer to see me after their extra classes on a Saturday I was hoping for maybe 25 or 30 youngsters to show up, so I was surprised when close to 100 arrived in the hall I was using for the session.

We started with a small exercise. For fear of being accused of plagiarism, I have to say I took this idea from an episode of *Law and Order: Special Victims Unit* that focused on teen bullying. Once everyone was seated and I'd explained that I wasn't there to lecture them, but they were there to talk to me, we began.

I asked them to close their eyes and take a moment to centre themselves. I told them it was essential that, for the exercise to work, they keep their eyes closed. By now you could have heard a pin drop, as they had no idea what would come next. I said, "I'm going to ask you to stand up if you've ever been hurt in any way by bullying." No one moved. I expected this as no one ever wants to be the first to admit to this. I said (in a friendly way): "I don't believe you. We've all been bullied at some point in our lives – I know I have." With this, just over half of them stood up. Then I asked them to stand up if they had ever been the victim of exclusion – being purposely left out of something, of a group. Another 10 or so stood. Then I asked anyone who had been the victim of gossip to stand up, and here some of the girls rose. Just once I had to remind them to keep their eyes firmly shut, which they did. Then the big one. Had any of them being bullied by way of sexual assault? Not one of those seated stood. Even though everyone's eyes were shut I think this was a step too far for them to admit. I quickly moved on to violence and a few more rose. Then I asked them to open their eyes, and as they did this I could see the surprise on their faces as they scanned around the hall to see nearly everyone standing.

I told them to look around and know that they're not alone, and that we're all in this together. Heads began to nod. I told them that they had the power to change bullying by being more accepting. I was now talking to everyone. I urged them all to be more compassionate and kind.

We then moved on to talking about their individual experiences, and again it took a while for them to open up. My first question to them all was, when they were bullied, did they go to their teachers? Here I got a resounding no, with just two students saying they did in fact go to their teachers. Most expressed anger at this scenario and said they felt their schools should address these situations. Some of the comments were:

- "We want to learn how to deal with being bullied, and how to handle the after-effects."
- "Schools only care about their own image" (something I heard from teens across the board).
- "No action gets taken against the bullies."
- "We want to know what punishments the bullies get – it's all hush-hush."

One student explained to me that in their school there was a lot of bullying, which the teachers knew about. "We can see that when it's not dealt with, it just gets bigger and can fester."

When it came to talking about social media, the atmosphere in the room suddenly changed and hands shot up, wanting to be heard. One girl said, with great passion, "I know we're all diverse, but no one has the right to hate speech, so if you say something and it offends someone, something should be done. If it's reported to Instagram, nothing will be done. We need for these issues to be given serious consideration."

Another student said, "We know now the school can't stop these types of bullying. We need stricter implementations with real consequences. Sometimes you hear of a bully that's been suspended, but that just means they'll be coming back and start their bullying all over again. Nothing changes. Everyone knows who the bullies are – they're the captains of sports teams. If we know who they are, why doesn't the school?" They explained to me how they would like to know just what punishments these bullies received. "You can't say they're being punished, but not tell us how. These bullies always say they'll stop bullying but we know words aren't enough."

One thing they all agreed on was that girls were worse bullies than boys. One student from an all-girls high school spoke about a particular social networking situation that happened at her school. "It started out as a page where people could post funny moments on, but it turned into an account that bullied people, with photos and even videos." This was made far worse by the latest addition to social media – confession pages, where apparently anyone can post anything about someone (true or otherwise). After numerous complaints to the school the page was taken down. But within days, she said, another page took its place.

What should teachers do?

Jorgensen explains that both schools and parents need resources to deal with these problems. "As a parent, you need to see that your child is a victim and decide what you're going to do about it. It's the same if your child is the bully. Most people explode and react, instead of responding to the situation.

"Just suspending a learner or giving them physical labour doesn't teach them anything. Kids need boundaries and structure but sometimes the punishment needs to fit the crime. There need to be consequences in place, but there also needs to be some sort of learning and understanding of what the repercussions will be. I tell learners to encourage their teachers to flip the switch and next time there's bullying, let the learners decide what the punishment should be. This is a huge deterrent for bullies as the learners will generally be far harder than the teachers. You need to get all the bullies into a room and do role playing, which we call social-emotional group learning or 'exploring the impacts'. It's important to give kids a voice – that's what they want and need."

According to Richards, bullying is a whole community issue. "If you're not dealing with parents, teachers and principals, you're not going to address the systemic issues. Unfortunately the fear of retribution is a major factor with high school learners when it comes to involving parents or teachers. They feel they'll be perceived as weak, needing their parents to intervene. This speaks to the shame and humiliation of bullying, which is just what bullying intends as its result. You can also find that parents, teachers and principals can be bullies themselves, which doesn't help the situation."

When nothing is done there's a risk of the bullied teen self-harming or attempting suicide, and often succeeding. Schools today have codes of conduct around bullying but the issue isn't so much whether these are put into effect, but how this is done. "If these rules aren't enforced calmly and constructively, things could get worse," explains Richards. "You can't bully a bully or threaten them. They're going to push back. If a mediation option isn't possible then the next step is to bring in the parents. If bullying was a teen's problem to solve we wouldn't have it, or it would be on a much smaller scale for adults to manage and resolve. A critical moment for intervention passes by and if nothing happens, it's like saying 'carry on bullying'..."

Identify

Perhaps the hardest part in the reporting of bullying, as mentioned earlier, is the "he said, she said" situation. Reporting will only be possible in a climate that allows people to speak up without fear of backlash or discrimination of any kind. No kid wants to be labelled a tattletale but knowing who and what you're dealing with is essential. "With bullying becoming so common an issue in schools, the word itself can easily be misused," explains Richards. "Minor misdemeanours like name-calling or eye-rolling is unpleasant, but shouldn't necessarily be classified as bullying. Bullying is systematic, repetitive behaviour. Very often, more serious violations are either not noticed or ignored by schools – some of which have a particular culture of bullying."

We've all seen the headlines that appear from time to time, particularly around initiations that go wrong at boys' schools. "This is simply interpersonal violence at schools where there's a culture of toxic masculinity. What makes this even harder to deal with is the added culture of not 'ratting' on others. This simply upholds this kind of bullying.

"With less resourced schools, you find youngsters coming into high school having experienced such high levels of personal violence at home or in their communities that they almost see it as a legitimate method of resolving disputes. There was another case in Limpopo where a food-queue jumping incident saw a pupil breaking a plate and then stabbing another with part of the plate. The school's answer, apart from immediate action, was simply changing the plates to plastic. What they need are *real* solutions. No one is asking, how can we reach youngsters early on to teach them how to resolve such issues without violence? The focus of bullying programmes is always on the perpetrators. The victim is maybe sent to hospital or receives social counselling by the Department of Social Development, but no one is looking at how to help people avoid becoming victims. To teach them to read the mood and act before a situation gets out of control," adds Richards.

Collect information

Even if you have to assure learners that their information will be kept confidential, gathering facts about an incident is always going to be a tough ask. Getting to the bottom of who did what can take time, but it's important to look deeply at each situation until you get the full picture. By using organisations such as FaceUp (their Facebook page offers anonymous online access to learners of schools who have subscribed to the platform), schools can make a practical difference. FaceUp's motto of "No one should be afraid to speak up" says it all.

I was constantly asked by those I interviewed to ensure that no one would know it was them. This, I realised, was a blend of helplessness and shame that these incidents had happened to them.

"We know that fear of telling someone about their bullying, particularly parents, is an issue," emphasises Lurie. "We need to empower our children by encouraging them not to keep what's happening to them a secret. They need to be able to tell someone they trust what's going on in their lives. Very often the child is scared that either they won't be believed by their parents or teachers, or even worse that they'll be labelled a 'snitch' – something that will live with them throughout their school years."

This was a common reaction from many of the teens I spoke to – fear of being labelled an informer or snitch, with the saying "snitches get stitches" being a constant in their school lives. Allowing learners to come forward anonymously can change this situation, giving power to people who feel they can't speak up. "You'll often hear stories of where a fight breaks out at school and a crowd gathers around, but no one does anything to stop it. Learners need to understand that being a bystander isn't cool. We need them to become 'upstanders' – everyday heroes," explains Jorgensen. "We tell them a bystander sees what's happening and by not doing anything, is as bad as the bully. By encouraging them to be upstanders and say this is not okay, and reporting these incidents, they must feel they're doing the right thing – taking a stand against bullying. This takes courage, action and assertiveness, with a dose of passion, which are the things we want to build in kids. To encourage them to say 'That's bullying'. If we don't give kids a means of speaking up in a safe way, this won't happen."

Know what you're dealing with

Say, for instance, you are faced with a case of online bullying, maybe sexual in its nature, you would have to understand how this world works before you could start becoming involved. If you work with teenagers, you have to understand their world.

This means comprehending the fast-changing social media whirl they live in, and what influences their choices and decisions. TikTok, Snapchat and Instagram came up constantly during my time spent with school children. Although I thought I understood just what these social networking applications were, when I spent several hours going through these sites I quickly realised how toxic and dangerous they can really be. Yes, users of these apps can show you how to put your make-up on properly, but they can also show kids what some random person – who just happens to be an "influencer" with zillions of followers – thinks is the perfect look. And if you don't match that look – obviously you're a loser. For the "loser" who refuses to or cannot fit into these moulds life can be tough – but at least if you try to understand what teens are experiencing in their online world, you'll be better equipped to start dealing with problems when they arise.

Some popular apps to know and understand are Instagram, Facebook, Snapchat, Twitter, WhatsApp, TikTok and Tinder.

Make sure your learners understand the risks involved in the social media world by addressing the following topics:

- Being wary of online strangers – never assume people are who they say they are.
- Being selective in who they follow, and who they allow to follow them.
- Discuss cyberbullying (Chapter 6 deals with cyberbullying in detail).
- Talk about sexting – which is classed as child pornography and is illegal for children under the age of 18.
- Discuss social media addiction.

Empower your learners

When you look at a school hall full of learners you'll see every type of child, from the bold and overbearing to the meek and mild, nerds, characters, and those who just want to be at school to learn and keep to themselves. So in other words: one size, when it comes to teaching about bullying, won't always fit all. But doing nothing and turning your back on what is obviously a problem is far, far worse. So how do you empower your students on an ongoing basis, and give them the tools and skills to be able to stand up for themselves and others whilst developing a culture of human rights in your school?

"I would like to see a bullying curriculum integrated into subject teaching at high schools," comments Richards. "This way you don't need an extra subject introduced, or people to come into school to give talks on bullying or interpersonal violence. Most of these people are completely out of touch on where adolescents are today. But if it's introduced by, say, an English teacher by way of debates around human rights, it would be very effective.

"What's needed is to educate kids around their rights and remedies. Explain that they can go to the police station and ask for protection. It's doable and there are organisations who can assist them, which automatically empowers them.

"They also need to understand certain dynamics. Who's going to target you? How do you manage this? Do you enlist a supportive therapist?

"What's important to keep in mind is that no two bullying situations are the same and each requires different interventions. In my practice and work with schools, I have enlisted the help of the police, particularly when nothing is being done elsewhere. Although this has often meant me being unpopular with schools, it's helped our collaboration in the long run and stopped certain bullying scenarios. Sadly, the bullies will go on to find other targets.

"When kids are given these long-winded speeches in assembly on bullying, they're generally a waste of time. The kids all know who the bullies are, and in fact the narcissistic bully gets excited by how the principal has now mobilised all these people into action through their misdoings. If you misdiagnose the perpetrator and put them into an improvement course, all they do is learn even more sophisticated psychological methods of putting other people down," states Richards.

Human aggression is never going to go away, so how do we deal with this from an early age? "Working with adolescents and young adults, I try to help them to see the 'shadow' side of themselves – that we all have the capacity for cruelty, intolerance, judgement, or aggression and violence. This is why just saying 'be nice to each other' in high school doesn't work – it's unrealistic," comments Richards. "We have to look at all these aspects of ourselves, acknowledge them, and not pretend you're in a better position to control these characteristics. So when we want to break the plate and smash it into the other person's eye, maybe we can say, perhaps this isn't such a good idea, let me regulate here. By learning and understanding your shadow and how to regulate it works far better than just telling someone to be kind, be nice. When learners hear this, most will be seen laughing behind their hands. We need kids to learn to be intolerant of intolerance, to be woke, as they say."

Schools must not be afraid to seek outside help from experts. It's not a failing on any school's part to admit there's bullying in its ranks. Rather do something before a learner takes their own life from the effects of bullying, and bring someone in. "I say to schools, if you find out a child is a bully that's a really important thing because just as much as the victim needs help, so does the bully," comments Jorgensen. It's not fun to be mean to someone. The fact they are potentially getting enjoyment out of it or that they're doing it in the first place is something that's not okay.

Jorgensen feels, "There need to be guidelines on how to keep both the bully and the victim safe within school grounds. What FaceUp does is to give learners an app – a space to speak up – and then ensures teachers are trained to deal with the types of reports that come in. Teachers are the first port of call when it comes to mental health and fears of suicide. If they don't have the tools and aren't equipped to handle situations, nothing will change."

Teaching tolerance

One of the least discussed topics in a country that needs constant debate in this area is tolerance. Of other cultures, races, belief systems, sexual orientations, disabilities, gender identities – the list goes on. Children's beliefs often echo their parents' skewed beliefs, having heard the same comments throughout their lives. In some homes, I would wager, many of these comments would indeed be classed as hate speech against anyone different, anyone that doesn't match up to what is considered "normal" and correct.

For Alison Gray, when it comes to tolerance, teaching by example is the way to go. "I was head of Grade 8 for 16 years and I felt like a mom to them. I knew all their names by the end of the second week and found we could talk openly and honestly about everything. We'd talk about just being kind and understanding differences. Then one day a Grade 10 learner wrote a really ignorant, thoughtless, racist WhatsApp post which his friends added to, even though the school had specifically addressed these issues with the learners. This literally brought the school to a standstill and we were all shocked. We think we teach tolerance, but if anyone really has the recipe I'd be glad to have it."

Once again, I could see a pattern emerging – why do some children show obvious empathy and tolerance, and some develop toxic behaviour towards others? The only reasonable answer I could find, and was told by many others, was simply: the apple doesn't fall far from the tree...

Gender and sexual diversity

A really big shift in schools over the past five years has been the change in attitude to **gender identity** issues, particularly when it comes to transgender and non-binary learners, and sexual orientation. In 2016 the Department of Basic Education published a booklet to help educators deal with homophobic bullying

> **gender identity:** an individual's self-perception as male, female and/or transgender.

called *Challenging Homophobic Bullying in Schools.*[11] This was produced to help educators make school grounds safer for learners across the LGBTQIA+ spectrum.

One segment of any school's student population open to intense bullying, without schools creating a safe space for them, are transgender learners. Transgender people's personal identity and gender doesn't correspond to the sex they are assigned at birth. Luckily, these days more schools are beginning to integrate such learners, as well as bring sensitivity and understanding of the issues involved, onto their campuses.

One such school is Westerford High, ahead of the pack when it comes to gender diversity. "We do have a group of transgender kids who want to be known by their own pronouns, whatever these may be – they or them, rather than he or she," explains Gray. "We're sending out a Google sheet this term to the whole school to say if you want a badge that indicates your preferred pronouns, fill in this sheet and then you can buy your badge.

"We also make provision for the learning of sexual identity and gender issues and let our learners choose a boy's or girl's uniform, whichever they feel comfortable wearing," says Gray. Westerford has a gender neutral bathroom, which other schools in South Africa are also installing.

These are, as you can imagine, tricky areas for schools to navigate and don't come without problems. Comments Gray, "What does trouble me, particularly with gender- and neuro-divergent kids, and maybe to a lesser extent race issues, is the level of sensitivity these kids have. It might be 'don't trigger me', 'don't say this, don't do that'. As much as you want to be sensitive to these issues, you can't sanitise the environment at school and never talk about these things. What would then happen to these kids when they get out into the big, bad world? This is exactly the environment where you should be triggered because you're surrounded by people who still care about you, who know your name, and will talk you through various things and support you. If we sanitise everything now, when you leave school and someone uses the wrong word, then what? It's a fine line to walk and we have to be building more resilience around this."

In most cultures, boys are supposed to play sports such as soccer and rugby; if they're more likely to hang out with girls or prefer drama to wrestling, they're often seen and condemned as homosexual.

Ron Addinall, clinical social worker, psychotherapist and an academic at the University of Cape Town, has over 20 years' experience working in the field of diverse sexualities and communities, as well as serving on the Transgender Clinic multi-disciplinary team at Groote Schuur Hospital. He is also a consultant to many schools in areas around gender diversity (where a person's gender identity, role or expression differs from cultural norms) and transgender issues.

Addinall is passionate about diversity and emphasises how far we have come in this area. "We're lucky to have one of the most liberal constitutions in the world, backed up by a legal framework which is very much on the side of the LGBTQIA+ community," he points out. However, this doesn't mean that every child who falls into this category has a smooth ride at school or in their community. "In the Western Cape where I'm based, the Department of Basic Education is busy drafting new legislation in this area, which will help schools formulate and put into practice policies which will clearly lay these out for the school community.

"Right now, the Schools Act says *all* young people have the right to education where they don't experience discrimination. This gives parents all the rights to confront any school they feel is not playing their part correctly here.

"Up to five years ago I would be approached by parents to help them navigate their queer, gender diverse or transgender child's journey at school and in the outside world. Today, with so many more young people coming out, schools contact me to come in and do workshops preparing teachers, school staff and learners around this topic. This means educating them around the various definitions of LGBTQIA+, and helping them through what can be a difficult area."

Even though most teachers and learners are fine with this and happy to embrace the topic and their fellow learners who fall into this group, there will always be those whose culture or religion will pose a problem. "You sometimes get a teacher, for instance, who without meaning to be insensitive, will say during a biology lesson that there can only be biological males and females. For a transgender boy or girl, this experience can be very triggering and exclusionary," explains Addinall.

One of the learners in the group I spoke to from the Alexandra Education Committee told me how certain teachers at her all-girls school make homophobic statements: "They would say 'boys and girls belong together', not 'girls can date girls' or 'boys can date boys'. If we say anything to support our gay friends [the teacher will] dismiss you completely."

Addinall says, "It's hard to break through hundreds of years of religious and cultural beliefs. I sometimes get learners come up to me and say how much they enjoyed my talk, but how their religious beliefs challenge what I'm saying. Being very mindful and respectful of this, I explain that while the religious doctrines are thousands of years old, we're talking about modern science and the breakthroughs that have been made in recent years, and it's just a good idea to open your mind to these also.

"One area where the internet really helps is allowing people to educate themselves on all these new terms they're confronted with. As parents of a child that comes to you as being gender diverse or transgender, the first thing you should do is some research around what they're telling you. All the information is right there on your computer, so there's no excuse for saying, 'I don't understand'.

"The main thing is to assure your child that you are one hundred per cent there for them. 'Unconditional love' isn't just words – it's real, and what any parent should always have for their child. This needs to be backed up by really listening to the child and hearing what their lived experience is, and how you as a parent can smooth the way for them. You are their ally and their advocate, whether this is intervening with their school principal or school governing body – whatever it takes. They need to know you're in their camp – on their team," concludes Addinall.

Tips for schools:

- Incorporate topics on bullying into the school's syllabus.
- Practice an open-door policy throughout the school, and make sure everyone is aware that an open-door policy exists.
- Let everyone know exactly what the school's anti-bullying policy entails. Discuss school policies with learners – it's likely they won't read them on their own.
- Allow open, anonymous reporting of bullying incidents.

- Try and establish facts around any bullying incident, while keeping an open mind.
- Be aware of areas in learners' lives that could be causing them distress or anger.
- Introduce a bullying prevention programme. This could include:
  - an anti-bullying learner committee;
  - a buddy system with a designated go-to person or place in the event of a bullying incident;
  - matric students adopting new learners to the school.
- Organise regular talks for teachers, learners and parents on diversity, kindness, bullying, and reporting and prevention of bullying.
- Help learners understand what may be funny to them isn't always funny to someone else – the line between teasing and bullying.

CHAPTER 4

Bullying in relationships

WHEN I BEGAN researching this chapter, I wasn't sure how many people would come forward and open up to me about their experiences of bullying in relationships. After posting a couple of requests on various social media pages, I was contacted by people from all walks of life with one thing in common: they'd all been in abusive relationships, and when I say abusive I'm not talking about the physical aspect, which isn't always the most painful part. I'm talking about the emotional hurt and humiliation deeply embedded in the stories that I listened to, and which I relay here.

I'm not naïve about just how common such relationships are, and when I look back over the years I can remember several times being invited to couples' homes for a meal and witnessing very real abuse, after which I'd wonder how any of them ever stayed together. These incidents of abuse weren't even hidden, with one partner (or even both) launching verbal attacks on the other, often after a few drinks. When the attacks were one-sided, they were often dismissed with "they're only joking". But you didn't have to look too hard to see the hurt lingering behind downcast eyes.

Generally when you hear the words "abused woman", you think of the colleague who comes to work wearing a scarf to hide her bruises. And yes, there are many more women than men who are physically abused – some to the point of dying, as we all too often read in newspaper articles, under the banner of gender-based violence (GBV).

There are even names for such circumstances – battered woman syndrome or battered person syndrome. The CDC (Centers for Disease

Control and Prevention) in the United States calls the type of abuse that occurs within a relationship intimate partner violence (IPV),[12] noting that intimate partner relationships can take many forms and can be applied to current or former partners, spouses, people who are dating, sexual partners and even non-sexual relationships; these can be heterosexual or same-sex.

Relationship abuse is a pattern of abusive and coercive behaviours used to hold power and control over a partner, which can be financial, sexual, emotional or physical.[13] Withholding access to a joint bank account, or dictating who you can and can't see or what you should wear, is highly abusive and can slowly turn a relationship into a prison sentence.

> **relationship abuse:** a pattern of abusive and coercive behaviours used to maintain power and control over a former or current intimate partner.

The hidden scars

Picture a beautiful woman, a business leader, dynamic within the work arena, respected by her peers and social circle. Now picture her in her home, nerves tightening and blood pounding through her head as fear grips her when she hears the garage door opening and her partner returning home. She – or possibly he, or they – are in an abusive relationship. Whether these bullies are labelled as narcissists, controlling or even psychopathic, we all probably know one – but possibly might never be able to identify them as such.

Many would think people in these situations must have a masochistic streak to stay in these brutal relationships – so why don't they walk out? According to author and life coach, Dr Renate Volpe, "It's the most complicated question you can ask. Relationship bullying can affect anyone, from any social or cultural background. What this means is that you can be financially independent, with your own career, and look to the world as though you have everything, but somehow walking out that door feels impossible."

Professor Renata Schoeman explains that you may see such couples and be impressed at how loving and caring they appear together. "Adult bullies have many faces, apart from just being the controlling romantic partner. In a relationship, such people often act loving and supportive as a way of keeping you in the relationship. But this doesn't make their abusive behaviour okay – it makes them a bully!"

It's worth repeating Schoeman's definition of relationship bullies from the introduction. Such people use bullying in relationships to instil fear, victimise or harass, whilst gaining power by taking their partner's power away from them. They have little regard for the consequences to a victim's health or well-being. "Quite simply, you don't have to hit someone to call it abuse," she says.

When working as a researcher and co-producer of a television programme on relationships a few years ago, our team recorded an episode on abusive relationships. We worked with a studio audience, who applied to be on the show, along with invited expert guests. During filming a very attractive lady, around the age of 50, stood up to tell her story. She related how, when her son and daughter were still young, she was in an extremely abusive marriage. She did everything she could to hide it from her children, but was worried how it would affect them in the long-term. The problem was that her husband wouldn't let her work and he had all the financial control. He also controlled who she could see and what she could wear, and eventually it became a case of having to get out of the relationship at all costs. She told of how one day, when he was at work, she took the children and ran away to a friend who'd offered to take her in. With no money of her own, she recalled how she would lie in bed with the children while she knitted socks and gloves to sell to get money for food.

As she was telling her story there was complete silence in the studio with all eyes focused on her face, which showed every emotion she had gone through at the time. When she'd finished, her twenty-something daughter who was sitting next to her stood up and, putting her hand on her mother's arm, said, "You've never told us why you left our father, and at the time we did resent you for it. Now I'm hearing what you went through, for the first time I really understand that you had no choice." This was such a raw and real experience that I will never forget it. I can only imagine how hard it was for both this mother and daughter to bare their souls in public like that. For the daughter, her father was someone she saw on the odd weekend when he would take her out and spoil her – a very different man to the one her mother had lived with.

A childhood sweetheart becomes a nightmare – Janet's story

The worst part is that no one really sees these alluring, charismatic people as a threat, even with warning signs, because they're so skilled at laying on the charm.

Janet[*], who as a teen was highly flattered by her new boyfriend Chris's[*] attention and focus on her, never thought for one moment this was anything other than love. From dating in high school, they became engaged at 19. At this point they were both at university – in different parts of the country.

"If I look back," explains Janet, a well-known and highly respected media professional, "the warning signs were already there. Going to varsity away from home should have been an exciting adventure, making new friends and taking part in campus life. I was particularly keen to become involved in the drama productions and the chamber choir, but this was impossible as rehearsals were at night and I had to wait for a call from Chris at 9 pm sharp every night at a particular telephone box on campus. This was before cell phones, but even if they had been around I would have had to be available at that time every night, otherwise I would get the third degree on where I was or what

I'd been doing. At first, this type of bullying wasn't so overt but I knew I had to be there for those calls."

This "obeying" of your partner's every request is a common thread in such relationships, points out clinical psychologist Ian Lipman. "Part of the bullying process is disempowering the other person. It's showing their assertion of self over someone else. Not all bullying is identical, it comes from different spaces and levels. Very often the bullies themselves have low self-esteem, and this is their way of finding their path."

"I'm a people pleaser by nature and as I promised Chris, I wrote to him every day and spoke each night," explains Janet. "When we got engaged everyone told me it was a bad idea, to which we both replied, 'You don't know what you're talking about.'

"In my fourth year at varsity our relationship fell apart. We'd argued over the phone, which just spurred Chris to get in his car and drive through the night to see me. He arrived and instead of smoothing things over, we had a big fight. He threw things at me, and when we spoke about it years later he said, 'But I deliberately missed you – I just threw it to frighten you,' which was far worse than doing something in an impassioned, impulsive way. This should have sounded a warning bell but it didn't. I broke up with him and his response was to bang on all my friends' doors in the middle of the night. This was followed by his mother phoning me to crap all over me for being a 'selfish bitch'.

"When I arrived home in Johannesburg, he came to see me and said he'd changed and worked on himself to never do anything like it again. And after this he seemed to be on good behaviour for a long time. By the time we were 23 we were married and everything was fine for a number of years – until gradually it wasn't."

At this point Janet goes quiet, and I see that retelling her story is having an emotional effect on her. "When I look back it's hard to pinpoint the bullying. There were small things, such as our very boisterous golden retriever who would burst into our two daughters' rooms as soon as he woke up. He just wanted to be with his family but Chris liked to sleep late, particularly on weekends when he was off. Small children and boisterous dogs didn't help here. Even my walking down the passage on our wooden floors would be too much noise for him. All this together made for drama – a hundred tiny dramas, where you get to the point where you can't constantly walk on eggshells any longer."

Janet was definitely going to try everything she could to keep her family intact. "A passion of mine is baking, and the only reason I started was because I would quietly get up at 5 am to sneak into the kitchen to keep the dogs quiet and stop them from waking up the kids and Chris. I'd happily miss out on my own sleep to keep the peace," she says, shaking her head and raising her eyebrows.

"I had wanted to go into a particular section of the media which I saw as exciting, but Chris, who was training in the world of science, saw our future fitting more around his wants. When I told him the field I wanted to go into, he quite simply said, 'You can't because you won't earn as much as I will, and someone has to earn the money in this household.' After this, his career was a priority with me trailing in his wake. This was just one of so many instances like that. He was always busy with his 'important' work, whereas anything I wanted to do was immediately dismissed, downplayed or actually insulted. If I dared to hold an opinion that was different to his, it was war.

"We didn't fight much, which wasn't a good thing. I would have to force myself to stay quiet even when I could see a train wreck coming. He'd grown up differently to me in that he found nothing wrong with borrowing money to buy large items such as cars – and he loved new cars. It was all about appearances for him. He'd show me elaborate calculations to prove we could afford it, and I knew we couldn't. At one point my parents were visiting and even when I clearly showed him I knew what I was talking about, he screamed at me in front of my parents, saying was I deaf or just stupid? This not only upset me and the children, but naturally my parents. He loved to cut me down in front of family or friends, including our children. He would encourage them to tease me, not in a loving way but one that would make me feel stupid. It's death by a thousand tiny cuts."

In Janet's case, after 22 years of marriage and a final decade of abuse, she decided to get divorced. This was, in her words, when the bullying kicked into full swing. "I had been feeling really terrible about myself and went to see a life coach who told me I was completely burnt out – emotionally, physically, spiritually – in every way there was to be totally exhausted. I'd been freelancing, while helping Chris in his business, looking after the children and doing a master's degree at the same time. He had all my support but I had nothing from him.

"Perhaps the worst part was the constant striving to keep him happy when he didn't want to be kept happy. I started to tweet and suddenly after 14 years finally found my voice again, and of course he didn't like this. I started talking and pushing back, setting tiny boundaries – which naturally he didn't take well."

As Janet gets to the turning point of her story, I see animation returning to her face. She tells me how she met a well-known South African musician online and when she mentioned to him that she used to sing and write songs, he asked her to send him some of them. "I said I couldn't possibly, but he persisted and I did. His reply thrilled me when he said they were better than quite a few professional musicians he dealt with. When Chris heard this he dismissed the whole thing and of course criticised my music."

The musician, however, didn't give up and with his encouragement Janet agreed to put on a concert in her garden where she would join him in entertaining family and friends. "I thought this was so generous, as we hadn't even met until then. I told Chris I didn't expect him to come and that if he wanted to, he could go out. On the day he lay on his bed sulking, refusing to come out, while I was busy hanging up lights. Eventually he managed to come and watch because he was 'being supportive'… He then proceeded to go through the garden criticising everything I'd done. While I performed he sat on a blanket with his back to me. People came and asked, 'Who *is* that man?' 'My husband,' I replied!

"He even came to me afterwards to tell me that my friends had said I'd done well – so well done. That was it – the last straw. This concert had meant so much to me, and he'd even managed to spoil that.

"For many years he'd been travelling for weeks on end for work, away from his family, not to mention going through all the fraud accusations against him – and for just one night he couldn't even be supportive.

"He'd actually lost so much contact with his children that when he would Skype them I would listen from the next room, and when I realised he was battling to find conversation would text him things to ask them. When he was home and we would have a family dinner, he'd just talk about himself and as soon as the children spoke he'd speak over them. It was exhausting.

"I'd already started making a life for myself and the children when he was away, taking them on road trips and doing fun things. When he returned, he angrily told me that he felt like an outsider in our marriage and wasn't included in anything. Our previous pattern had always been that he would accuse, I would apologise and assure him I'd never do it again, and adjust myself so that I'd never be accused of that thing again.

This meant walking on eggshells all the time." For Janet there was now no going back, but getting out wasn't straightforward.

Janet and the girls now live in a far more modest home in a less affluent suburb, but they have something no money can buy – freedom, peace and happiness. "It took me so long to finally relax. I hadn't realised how exhausting my life had been. I even had to have treatment for post-traumatic stress disorder. Getting maintenance out of him is still a grind each month, often seeing me have to pay for varsity fees and monthly expenses. Meanwhile he lives in his palatial house with his new wife, changing his cars on a regular basis. I'm waiting for the inevitable call from her in the next few years. You can only keep up a façade for so long."

Janet was someone I knew as a colleague but we had never been in each other's social circle. She always appeared to be a super confident, highly professional person, so I was surprised at her story.

Being a people pleaser is a common thread in these stories. As Volpe explains: "It all centres around the personalities involved. You've got your codependent, who is a mix of compassion and empathy, with their choice in life being, 'I wouldn't want anyone to suffer in life as I've done,' so they pre-empt others' pain and intervene and assist. This is generally mistaking love for being needed. You often find their partners are narcissists who possibly come from an abusive or indulgent background, with limited empathy and compassion. Their attitude is, 'I don't care about any of you – I'm out here for myself and am entitled. Get in my way and I'll crush you.'"

According to Joshna Lutchman, social worker and head of operations at FAMSA (The Family Life Centre of South Africa), "The biggest challenge for women in abusive relationships is leaving their partners. They have no idea where to start or where to go. Eventually, if they feel their life and their children's are in danger, they will flee. We have women come to us who are in relationships with very wealthy partners, who give them a good life materially but who rule over them like mafia warlords. Their every move is monitored: where they go, who they see. They desperately want to leave but can't see a way out."

This view is endorsed by Volpe. "If you try and divorce a narcissist, you're dealing with the devil – people driven by sabotage and revenge, who get pleasure out of inflicting pain. They'll do anything to you or use your children to hurt you. Sadly, when you do go to court the judge will take the upstanding man of the community's side..."

As women, we often grow up with this fairy-tale idea of the perfect romance, the perfect marriage resulting in the perfect family, and a perfect life. The reality check is that this is far from the truth – even for the happiest of marriages. But when you're young and starry-eyed, romance still wins out.

Losing yourself – Thulani's story

Thulani* was 28 when she was swept off her feet by the man she thought to be her real-life prince – straight out of a fairy tale. Nothing was too much for him, from encouraging her studies and recommending books, to looking through her assignments. He was interested in everything about her and her family and she was bowled over by his attention. She'd never met a guy like this, and before long they were married and had their first child. "During the pregnancy he was still quite helpful, watching what I ate, making sure I had enough protein and vitamins, even attending antenatal classes," explains Thulani. But as soon as the baby was born the fairy tale ended.

"Almost overnight he became a different person – a very rude one. Even though I knew he liked a drink, suddenly this became a daily after-work exercise. At weekends, instead of spending time together he'd be 'sleeping it off'. When I'd question him, asking where he'd been or when he was coming home, I'd be told he was the head of the house and didn't have to answer to me. I realised that it was one of his ways of controlling me and manipulating me into silence – it was all mind games. Everything came down to me, how I was judgemental and selfish. I actually started to believe his rhetoric – that perhaps I was selfish.

"Then he suggested I stop working – another way of controlling me. I refused as I'd already been bored stiff during four months' maternity leave." He then laid down the ultimate guilt trip, telling Thulani how his mother had always been home for him, and that he earned a far bigger salary than she did anyway.

Things went from bad to worse for Thulani, with the drinking becoming heavier and his initial perfect-man façade completely disappearing. As she speaks to me her voice becomes weaker as though she's taking herself back in time, to a place where she lost herself. "After the baby was born, his sister passed away and his friends told me to give him a break as he was grieving. He started becoming aggressive and I didn't want to argue in front of the baby. Somehow, I thought once he'd stopped grieving he'd go back to being a normal person again but instead things became much worse."

We've all been shocked at some point when we pick up a newspaper or see an online article about a well-known personality who is a wife-abuser. "What? That can't be possible," we say. "They seem so nice on television!"

"When outsiders hear one partner accuse the other of abuse, particularly when the man is good looking and charming, they will find it hard to see him as an abuser. It's often the wife who's seen as the bad one who can't make the marriage work," explains Volpe.

When his father was diagnosed with cancer, Thulani's husband decided he wanted to have a second child so his dad could have time with his grandchildren. The decision had nothing to do with their relationship or marriage, but was purely to please his father. "Our entire marriage was around him trying to please his parents," says Thulani, tensing as she speaks.

Thulani became pregnant and the drinking continued. Then she started seeing messages on his phone that told her he went from one bar to the next, often with women involved. "This was after I looked at his search history and found porn, porn and more porn. His answer was, 'So you were looking for it, and now you've found it.' I asked if there was a problem in our marriage, to which he replied by saying the porn was just something he did, and that if we had enough sex he wouldn't need to do this."

From there, Thulani went on to try what so many women in this situation have done before her – become the perfect wife and perfect mother. "I tried everything, but he didn't change a thing. I was always trying to fix things as I thought I was the problem. Now with children only 22 months apart, I'd ask him if he couldn't come home early to help me a little and have dinner with the children, who would ask where he was. His reply was that if I needed help he'd pay our domestic worker extra to stay late. This also made him angry and, as usual, I'd feel bad and stay quiet."

To his friends and family he would appear the perfect husband, particularly when they'd visit, seeing him bathing, feeding and playing with the children. "He would nurse his hangover every Saturday morning before magically appearing outside, cleaning the yard and doing the garden – appearing for our neighbours to be a dream husband with a perfect family. That was the face he wanted to portray to the world. Once the doors closed behind us, I would go back to tiptoeing around him again."

Even though Thulani knew there were now other women involved, she was too frightened to say much as the barrage of verbal abuse she would get just made things worse. When World Aids Day came around she saw a chance for them to at least get tested for HIV. "I took this opportunity around a rare time that he was trying to please me, as he'd said he wanted to do better. We did the tests that were negative, which just led him to fresh abuse about the fact I thought he'd been unfaithful. I didn't think it – I knew it."

Having her family or friends around was now becoming too painful. To have to watch every word she said, or not to raise an eyebrow at the wrong time. Her food – which she took great pains over, even asking a chef at work to help her with her cooking – was mocked, with Thulani once again feeling a failure. "By now my friends and family had noticed the change in me, seeing through his act when they visited, which became less and less. Once, he discovered from a friend's husband that I'd talked about him to her, and again I was lambasted – how could I criticise him to a friend? When his family visited he was really on form. He'd say I hadn't cooked enough – was I trying to starve them and our children? Not one of his family would say a word and I realised they were just like him. I also realised that it wasn't just verbal abuse that hurt so badly – but that silence was just as deadly. It was so much better to have no one around, which led to me feeling more and more isolated.

"Social media was out, as he monitored anything I posted. I didn't dare post that I'd been out with friends for lunch and had a good time."

I asked Thulani what the proverbial straw was that broke the camel's back? "There were so many, but I think it was when he started sharing photos of our children with a woman I knew he was seeing, that I had to do something. I didn't want to deprive my children of a father, and I still believed I could save our marriage at this point. After doing some research and speaking to a therapist and our pastor, I suggested marriage counselling. This was met with the answer that he didn't want people meddling in our affairs – it wasn't the African way. So we settled on having family members as our counsellors but he continually tried to delay this by putting the problem of travelling to meetings into the mix, which he knew I couldn't do with the children."

"Why, knowing that he was having an affair, did you still stay?" I ask. Thulani looks down and shrugs, shaking her head as tears form in her eyes. "It was so hard."

As Lutchman says, "Even though many women are so abused by their husbands who are busy having other relationships, these women simply suck it up because they still don't want to be left alone – particularly with children."

And then the bombshell was dropped on Thulani when her husband said, "'You know that culturally the children belong to me, so I'm going to take the children.' I was on the verge of having a panic attack and called my mom crying, telling her he's going to take the children. She assured me that without my consent he couldn't do this and that they'd have him arrested if he tried, but that didn't help the fear he'd instilled in me with this threat."

It was shortly after this that a friend who she hadn't seen for a long time spelt out the truth for her. "She couldn't hide the shock on her face when she saw me, but when she said the words that I was 'a mere shell' of myself, that I knew I had to get out of this marriage permanently."

Naturally this wasn't a smooth process and by now physical abuse had begun, which culminated in a late-night call to the police. "He came home drunk and banging on the door. I begged him not to wake the children but of course that didn't worry him. He wanted them to be awake, and asked them if they knew what a witch was. When they said no, he pointed to me and said their mother was a witch. By now I'd called the police, who arrived, taking in the scene immediately; it was nothing new to them. He was just as belligerent to them as he was to everyone else and eventually he opted to leave the house rather than be arrested. After spending the night sleeping in his car, he packed his bags and left."

Although their divorce is still not finalised, Thulani has finally managed to move on with her life. She explains that it's magic just to hear her children laugh – something she wasn't used to – as well as not having those eggshells to walk on. "Not surprisingly, when he has the children every other weekend he plays the perfect father, playing with them and buying them presents. My friends come to visit me and marvel at the house that now feels like a home."

As I listen to Thulani's story and see the emotions cross her face, the thought occurs to me that I'm hearing similar stories on this topic from all my interviewees. But I'm sitting here with this wonderful, self-assured woman who couldn't possibly be the same person in this story? After all, there's nothing pathetic or remotely stupid about her – quite the opposite.

"No one could believe my story when they heard it. That's why I'm talking to you now," explains Thulani. "If I can stop just one person going through what I went through, it's worth it. My life is so different now. Simple things make me realise what I went through. Just being able to buy my favourite fruit juice, which I didn't have for years, is so freeing. Imagine that..."

Spotting the narcissist

The word narcissist comes to mind when I listen to these people's stories. Dr Volpe explains to me that it's actually very easy to spot a narcissist. "They have a repertoire of 15 to 17 behaviours, divided into covert and overt narcissism. Overt is the easier to spot – it's all about me, me, me and I! Very often they'll be leaders, charismatic people who at the same time are often predators with a tremendous amount of pride. TV-show pastors come to mind here. One thing they all have in common is that they'll be charming – until you get in their way.

"The covert one is far more dangerous – the teddy bear. They appear to almost be victims, making you feel sorry for them and rescue them. You've got to listen to every bit of their conversation, while they never listen accurately. They can't identify with your emotions. They're difficult to spot because they will emulate just what you need, hooking you in – now known as 'love bombing' – until they have you. They'll just as easily **gaslight** you, making you doubt your sanity. They'll bully and even threaten you – all covertly, and very subtly.

> **gaslight:** to manipulate someone using psychological methods into questioning their own sanity or powers of reasoning.

"For people who come from a home where the father only had to raise an eyebrow to get your attention and often made you recoil in fear without raising a finger, the likelihood you'll get involved with someone just like that is very real," concludes Volpe.

This was exactly the scenario for Angie*, whose dysfunctional home life led her to think she'd never want to be like that. And then she met Paul*.

"It could never happen to me" – Angie's story

For anyone who knows Angie, they would agree: an extremely energetic, positive person who gives her all to anything she's faced with, she is the epitome of a highly successful woman. But often this is the public persona and not the private one.

Angie grew up in a home where, despite her father being abusive to her mother, they were married for 56 years. "He wasn't abusive to us, just emotionally absent. I never had that father-daughter bond, which meant I always had a detachment issue. I saw my dad abusing my mom and built a wall between him and me, telling myself that I'd never marry a man like that. And then I did..."

On paper, Angie and her husband Paul seemed the perfect couple. They were both involved in the church, had lots of friends, were sporty, and he was involved in mission trips. "He seemed like he was my guy," explains Angie.

Coming from a religious background, Angie grew up hearing the Bible's words: "Wives, submit to your own husbands as to the Lord."[14] But she never anticipated how literally her new husband took this phrase. "My 'normal' was seeing how my father treated my mother, add religion to this and I thought it must be true if it says this in the Bible. Subconsciously my mind was looking for someone familiar – no one *looks* for an abuser."

It wasn't long into the marriage that the emotional and financial abuse began. "Paul would make me put my salary into his account, with him managing our finances – because that's what the man of the house does. Every month I'd give him all my money, and if I spent anything I'd have to justify where I spent it. He earned less than me but held the purse strings.

"As a man, if he did anything wrong it was just a normal bloke being naughty thing, but if I had stepped in any way out of line, I was a sinner. Sex before marriage and drinking, according to Paul, made me a sinner. Within a short space of time he went from being the social person I'd first gone out with to becoming insular, saying our marriage is private and we must solve any problems we have together. When I spoke to my mom, she'd say he's just like your dad, so I guess I was just keeping the abuse cycle going."

They do say love is blind, and even when there are numerous warning signs of danger before a marriage, there's very little chance of stopping it. "His mom said to me, 'Wow, you're going to marry this boy – and you're going to want to give him back.' I thought, what a dreadful thing to say. He quickly told me that his mother had never loved him, which I found out meant he had mommy issues. His parents quickly saw that things were starting to go wrong in the marriage and they said I needed to get help. As far as Paul was concerned, his life was fine and always had been. There were times he'd admit to being abusive and change for a short while – before soon going back to his old self."

At this point in the interview, I ask Angie why she hadn't got out of the marriage then. She turns away, self-consciously. "It was simple – I really wanted to be a mom. We spoke and things seemed to be getting better, and quite quickly I found I was pregnant. My pregnancy went really well but I had the most awful postnatal depression [PND]. It wasn't really surprising, as during my pregnancy Paul told me what an awful mother he thought I'd be. Having had anxiety in my family, I'd asked my gynaecologist if I was likely to have PND. She said, 'No way, you're so confident and together, healthy and happy.' The birth was quite traumatic and I ended up having a caesarean section. Somehow after that I lost all my confidence and ended up being hospitalised. Paul assured me that he'd be there and look after our daughter, Jessica*. I felt like a basket case – which totally suited him. He wanted me to be completely reliant on him. This went on for a long time, and by the time Jessica was two I had a relapse."

All through her marriage, Angie held on to the hope she could make it work. She admits that she did love Paul and wanted her marriage to last, which to most people reading this would seem strange. "Relationships go through biological stages," explains Ian Lipman. "There's the initial romantic stage and then the hormonal phase, which is very real. This is probably where the saying 'love is blind' comes from. They have actually done biological research which shows how these hormones change over the years in a marriage.[15] These initial high levels of hormones only last three to four years and then the romance phase is over. This is why living together is a good idea – if you can get through those first few years, you're more likely to see your marriage survive," he confirms.

A few years later, Angie was offered a prestigious bursary to study for three weeks at a top university in the United States, which Paul strongly objected to. "He felt my place was at home, looking after him and my daughter. His words were: 'I'm not going to allow you to go!' The organisation I worked for insisted I take this opportunity up, so he backed down and even joined me afterwards for a holiday."

Volpe explains that this is called intermittent reinforcement. "Nobody can be all dark. They can also be charming. When they feel things are going their way, there will be holidays and good times together. They want to be seen as positive people. The minute you go into their territory of what they need or want, or you make them feel inadequate or shame them, make them feel guilty – that's when the demon comes out," she explains.

After her trip to the USA Angie's career went from strength to strength, and the more successful she became, the harder her home life became. "Paul was very aware of the disparity in our jobs – mine really going places and his nowhere. I realised I'd be the one who had to work as well as look after Jessica. I was like a single mom who was married."

In a patriarchal society such as ours, women who are more successful than their husbands are still not readily accepted. Volpe explains, "Women can be top professionals at work and then come home and lose the ability to stand their ground, command respect and cope with the dynamics in their own households. But they'll deny their pain and cover up their loneliness to maintain a façade for others. Lives become devoid of joy and meaning, purpose and passion, merely surviving, while attempting to hold marriages and families together."

Things only got worse for Angie, with occasional physical bullying but mostly swearing and rages. "Paranoia became the order of the day and he was convinced I was having an affair, which was far from the truth. The effect this had on Jessica saw her going from a happy toddler to an anxious, clingy four-year-old. She was like a little mouse. In order not to ruffle any feathers and keep things calm at home I put a lot into being a perfectionist, which was exactly what I'd done as a child when my dad became abusive. Somehow, I still thought it better for Jessica if we stayed together."

Fast-forward another few years and things really started escalating – badly – and Angie managed to convince Paul to see their pastor. "[The pastor] told me he was worried that Paul's abuse was 'off the charts', and that if I couldn't get him to come and see him, they were going to see how to protect me or get me out of my situation. Paul eventually agreed to see this pastor, who asked him some really poignant questions. Afterwards, the pastor told me he thought Paul was a sociopath. He'd told the pastor he'd fix things and that he wouldn't come to see him again. When I heard this I remember almost having a panic attack. My last hope of help had vanished, I thought."

At that time Angie had to fly to New York for a few nights and her sister, who lived in California, flew in to spend a couple of those nights at the hotel with her. When she returned home, Paul was waiting and confronted her, asking who had been with her at the hotel. When the reply was her sister, he dismissed it as being too convenient an answer. With that, he threw her out of the house.

"He kept Jessica, telling her that I was useless and an adulteress. He added that I was just focused on my career and had met someone else, so she would now stay with him. Ironically, I went to stay with his parents who were totally on my side, eventually getting a restraining order against him. By this time he'd done a good job of manipulating

Jessica, telling her that if she lived with me she'd be left on her own at home, and if I met someone else she'd be totally ignored," Angie recounts.

Eventually Angie had no choice but to seek police intervention, who arrived at the house to get him to leave. "When the police told Jessica to come with me, she refused, saying her dad had said I would just go to work all the time. Jessica and I were very close, so I knew something very psychological was going on. For the second time I found myself in front of a magistrate, who this time said that we had to get Paul out of the house as he felt both Jessica and I were in danger. Now I found myself returning home with the police escorting me. When we arrived, there was Paul cooking dinner for Jessica like super dad, not even bothering to acknowledge the fact that the police were in his kitchen. His response was that this was the second time I'd called the cops, and that didn't they know I'd had postnatal depression and was 'a little cuckoo'. Jessica was also furious with me and wanted to know why I was breaking up the family. He'd been feeding her his brand of anti-mom propaganda."

Once the police had in fact removed him from the house, Paul's problem became where to go, as his parents had told him that he couldn't go to them as he was so abusive. "That's when he realised he had a real problem. He messaged me saying he was a narcissist and was sorry for the abuse he'd piled on me, but that I must be patient!"

It's hard to believe but Angie agreed to counselling, under the condition that she and Paul would separate, which they did for a year, with him moving to a rental property they owned. "Our couples' therapist said it would have been easier if he'd had an affair as it was easier to fix than an abusive marriage."

Angie was then headhunted for an even more prestigious job that meant going to Canada for four weeks. Even though their therapy continued whilst she was overseas, when she returned Paul's first words were that Jessica was going to stay with him for longer, as Angie was the worst mother on earth. This was despite initially having supported her in the decision to change jobs. "That was when the last iota of hope and love left me," says Angie, in a voice reflecting her dejection at the time. "I thought, this is never going to change, this is it." Straight after this, Angie filed for divorce.

Naturally, Paul tried to make the process as difficult as possible, citing Angie as the bad, workaholic mother. Luckily for Angie a friend had advised her to record her interactions with Paul, particularly when he was on a screaming tirade. "The one I had was him screaming at Jessica: 'Why did you open the drawer?', 'Why didn't you lock the door?', 'Where's the...' Never anything of consequence. In the recording you can also hear him saying to an 11-year-old Jessica, 'I'm going to fuck you up.' You can also hear him pushing me, and me landing badly."

This recording became Angie's trump card and her lawyer immediately sent it to Social Development, who said this was grounds for immediate removal of Jessica from her father. "When social workers arrived at the house Paul refused to open the door. Jessica was screaming and asking why I was doing this, causing trouble again with her dad. He was telling her the social workers were going to put her in an orphanage, which is why she didn't want to go with them. They managed to convince her that this wasn't the case, but nevertheless it was over an hour of Paul screaming at me through the door.

"I felt like I was on a *Jerry Springer* episode – it was so surreal." For Angie, it was a case of survival. She told me she didn't feel sad, she just felt numb. "Later, Social Development did an investigation of Paul and said that he wasn't a drug addict or alcoholic, and was only abusive when I was around, so we signed a co-parenting agreement with Jessica staying with each of us for a week at a time. They did warn me, though, that they felt that as Jessica got older he would probably start abusing her too, and that if we needed help to call them."

This new arrangement didn't last for long before Paul once again refused to let Jessica go to her mother. "This time Jessica began to tell me he was abusing her, shouting at her and accusing me of lying. She didn't want to stay with him any longer."

From here the legal journey for Paul would have been to force his daughter to stay with him, which even he recognised as being wrong. Today, Jessica refuses to stay with Paul and both she and Angie have had therapy. Angie is working to understand her complicit role in staying in the marriage for 15 years. "There were all those triggers that kept me in the marriage. I don't know why I didn't speak out. I almost saw it as my lot in life. If I look where I am now, it's a different life. I trail ride, go hiking and don't have to tiptoe around anyone just to get through the day. Jessica has her horse and riding, which has been a big part of her healing. In some ways I felt like a refugee, rescued from a war zone where the choppers were overhead and dropping the odd food parcel. On a daily basis I feel relief and gratitude. I don't have any bitterness or resentment – I just want to move on with mine and Jessica's lives." When I ask Angie about meeting someone else, I see her expression change and become guarded. "Maybe I'll meet someone but right now I'm definitely not looking for a relationship. I'm just enjoying the life I have now."

Confronting the past

Although we generally think of the many women who fall into the category of abused in relationships, there are, of course, many men who have also been down this dark and sometimes dangerous road. One such man, who has taken what was an abhorrent situation and made use of it to help and educate other men, is Martin Pelders.

Not only women are abused – Martin's story

I visit Martin Pelders at the Randburg branch of his non-profit organisation, MatrixMen, an awareness and peer support group for male survivors of sexual abuse – which often goes hand in hand with bullying. More and more, I was hearing stories of adults who'd lived with abuse for such a large part of their lives that they absorbed internally, whilst their feelings came out in other ways. For Pelders, this became a-bottle-a-day alcoholism. "By the time I was in my mid-twenties, I was struggling with booze, depression and suicidal ideation. This was my life and it never struck me that something was wrong," he explains.

It wasn't until he found himself facing a mid-life crisis in his forties that he had his wake-up call, and was forced to confront his life and the role bullying and sexual abuse played. "After totally embarrassing myself and my family at my younger brother's fortieth birthday, I realised things had to change. Although the first few months were tough, I managed to stop the excessive drinking. But what was worse was that I had to face my depression sober."

He'd tried Alcoholics Anonymous, which didn't work for him, and he knew each day things were becoming more unbearable. "In 2010, I came home early from work and *The Oprah Winfrey Show* was on TV. My wife said, 'You'd better watch this,' taking my daughter and leaving me to watch on my own. The next 60 minutes changed my life. There was Oprah, talking about a group of men 2 000 miles away in Chicago who could have all been me, living my life. Some of these men were in the studio with her.

"At the end of the programme one guy said, if you're a father, I promise that you would never hurt your children or do anything damaging to them. Even though you've been a victim of sexual abuse, you can be a good father. These words slapped me around the face and I broke down. At the same time, the memories it evoked were really painful and I hadn't realised how deep I'd buried these inside me. I could remember every detail of those encounters, those rapes, visually and mentally. But it took this experience, watching *Oprah*, for me to move on and grow. I'll always be grateful for that," says Pelders, the tears pricking at his eyes as he tries to control his emotions.

His entry into a world of bullying and abuse started from very young. "I grew up in the era of children being seen but not heard, so when this woman started to sexually abuse me from the age of five, I didn't know how to get people to believe me and I didn't know how to say no to an adult! When I did try and tell my parents or other people about this, my comments weren't really listened to and simply dismissed. With fights and a cold war playing out at home, I didn't realise until years later that my dysfunctional family wasn't normal. To me, the abuse I was exposed to was normal and I thought it was part of being a kid. This was my normal.

"It was only when a Swiss family moved in next door to us and I began to spend time in their house, that I saw what a normal family was like. When I asked if they'd adopt me, they just laughed. They didn't realise I was serious.

"By the time I was a teenager, and this abuse and more was still happening to me, my mood swings and anger were put down to the fact that I was a normal teenager. This just strengthened my belief that obviously my opinions didn't count."

What wasn't normal for a 13-year-old was the bottle a day of alcohol that Martin's friend introduced him to. Even though it burnt at first when he was drinking it, the feeling that let him forget all his pain and problems was worth every drop. Add to this his undiagnosed depression and the suicidal thoughts, and you had a life out of control. Regular car and bike accidents were a result, and even five suicide attempts never rang the warning bells that something was seriously wrong.

By the time Martin was 16, he just wanted to be out of his home as much as he could. So when he met a charming man in his forties who promised a life of speedboats and plane rides, Martin found it hard to resist. What he didn't realise was that he was being groomed – by a clever paedophile. "Before long he had a real hold over me, manipulating me to get what he wanted, telling me that if I didn't do what he wanted he'd report my parents to the police. I didn't know any better, but knew I didn't want my dad to go to jail. Neither he nor I were gay, but he just liked little boys. And after reading some papers I found in his house, I realised he was also a con man. This explained the boats he would buy and the flying lessons he would take me for.

"There was, of course, a price to pay. This would be making me sleep over at his house with him next to me. I felt I had no control over any of this. He would take me to parties at this woman's house where there were all sorts of really weird people, and my eyes nearly fell out over what I witnessed happening there. I was just another plaything to these people."

It would be many years before Martin could cut this man out of his life, but then he found himself jumping from the frying pan right into a fire. "I got married to a woman who was also completely controlling. We went on to have a daughter, and I was so scared of doing anything untoward to her that I'd always leave the door open if I was bathing her or changing a nappy. I was super aware of this situation and terrified I'd want to do something I'd regret. This never leaves you."

This marriage ended and again Martin found himself depressed, alone and with only alcohol to comfort him. In time he met a woman who began to make him feel whole again – but he wasn't totally there. "All my life I knew I wanted what I didn't have – the perfect family, living in a comfortable house, with everything that goes with that. The sad thing is that even when I did have all this, it didn't help how I felt about myself and life. I was angry – a lot – and this was real rage. I hated that I felt like this but didn't know how to stop."

Until Martin saw that life-changing *Oprah* show. From there, he started seeking answers and a way forward. Finding real help for the first time in his life and people who really listened to him, he managed to start afresh. "Today I eat properly, exercise regularly, and use other methods to come to terms with my life and what happened to me. My wife and I also adopted a baby who's the centre of our world, and I finally have that dream I was looking for."

But for Martin, his recovery prompted him to help others whose stories were similar to his, particularly male survivors of sexual abuse. "I knew there were a lot of guys out there like me, who had nowhere to turn, particularly here in South Africa. That's why, in 2011, I started MatrixMen, which has gone on to help so many others. We run counselling and groups where we have guest speakers and also encourage people to talk out, to help people understand how common sexual abuse for men actually is."

FAMSA also sees an increasing number of men who are in abusive relationships. "This seems to be on the rise," comments Joshna Lutchman. "Men struggle to share their stories and rather internalise them. When they go to the police, the reaction is generally one of disbelief. Our police are rarely trained to deal with any marital issues. This is a big problem and one that needs addressing. People, especially men, are reluctant to go to the police as they feel they are victimised further rather than offered empathy and real help."

Peeling back the layers – Wendy's story

Like Martin, Wendy* came from a home where she felt emotionally neglected but not abused, although she describes her father as her "first bully". As one of eight children with the church a prominent part of their lives, being sent to youth camps from young was a gateway to problems. "I started having serious relationships with boys from the age of 13, although sex wasn't involved – just 'snogging'," as Wendy points out to me. "Seventeen-year-old Luke's family went to the same church as we did, with his parents being missionaries. Coming from a physically and emotionally deprived background, I had no idea about loving relationships. My parents loved me, they just didn't know how to show it. We were brought up by nannies and by Grade 1, I was already catching the bus to school on my own."

One thing Wendy was sure of was that she wanted the whole fairy-tale romance and wedding – the perfect home and kids. And that was what she thought she was getting. "Sadly," explains Dr Volpe, "dreams of finding your knight in shining armour rarely turn out that way. Very often disillusionment will upset the marital bliss. Once lust has diminished, fairy-tale dreams don't happen. Young couples need to have the ability to demonstrate respect, empathy and compassion towards one another."

By the time Wendy was 20, she and Luke were married. What she didn't know was that she was going from a childhood devoid of warmth to an equally scary and emotionless marriage. "When I became aware he was emotionally and psychologically abusing me, I would hear myself screaming but only on the inside."

Married for 28 years and now separated for four, only the last few years have seen Wendy being able to peel back the layers of her life to find herself.

"Looking back, Luke never even really asked me out. We'd gone on a walk with some friends and he just took my hand – that was his way. When he decided I would be his girlfriend he didn't have to ask me, he just took it for granted. He's never had social skills – taking my hand was, to him, my agreement to go out with him. He'd fetch me from school and somehow was constantly there. When I look back now I see there were a lot of red flags, which I was unaware of then. Had I understood their meaning I would never have married him."

This statement resonates with Lutchman. "Everyone likes attention paid to them. With these guys it comes so easily. Whether it's child or adult abuse, it's all about luring your prey in and then grooming them. It's so easy to fall for it and then be ensnared."

When you think that Wendy was only in her teens at this point, it's easier to understand how she was led on by Luke's attentions and even his outrageous behaviour. "One day my younger brother was on the back of Luke's bakkie, which at that age he thought was great, when Luke suddenly swerved into a car park with my brother going flying through the air and landing bruised and cut on the ground. Instead of taking my brother home or to get help, Luke left him in the car alone, bleeding and crying, while we went into the shops for an hour. I still have nightmares about that day. My parents predictably did nothing. I'd grown up around emotionally numb parents, and then I married one.

"I'd seen the way my father treated my mother, the mind games and the belittling, demeaning her in a friendly way people couldn't see through. The covert bully is far worse than the one who throws punches. Those you can see coming.

"From the first day, the control never let up. Even when it came time for me to work, Luke decided I had to work at a particular bank where I could get a staff loan – and after going from bank to bank I eventually did just that. But from the very first pay cheque it went straight into his account, with me having to put my hand out and ask for whatever I wanted."

Once they had their first child it was decided by Luke that Wendy would stay home with the baby. "This wasn't really a grand gesture by him, but yet another way to make me dependent on him. After three miscarriages I desperately wanted something to fill an empty space within me, so when our daughter was 13 we adopted another daughter, Nthabi*. This also suited Luke, because he now had me home where he wanted me. If I tried to start a new hobby that took me anywhere at night, I'd be accused of not wanting to be married. He wasn't supportive of anything I'd do outside the house.

"What I only realised later was that adopting Nthabi was as much about his image to the outside world as anything else. To show everyone what a good thing he'd done. He worked in finance for a large retail organisation and also liked to sit on boards. He'd be on them for a short time before he became chairman. He loved the attention and getting awards. His aim was for us to look like the perfect family."

"So often when people look from the outside at a relationship, they see the ideal couple in a loving marriage. The husband will be attentive to his wife's every need," explains Lutchman. "It's the subtle, emotional aspects that stay hidden. Often the abuse has been so traumatic that it can take 35 years before they will speak out and eventually move on."

Although Wendy did break up with Luke after finding him cheating on her, she took him back. "Things just got worse with him criticising everything and telling me to lose weight – body shaming me. I'd say to him I'd rather he punched me than say these things, as bruises will heal but words won't." By 2015, Wendy suspected once again that he was having an affair. "He would pick fights with me to justify his behaviour because then I'd get mean, and he'd belittle me in front of my daughters in public. We'd be in a restaurant and I'd suggest something for Nthabi to eat. He'd jump in and say she would eat what he said and how dare I question him in front of the kids. He liked to discipline me like a child, telling the kids what a stupid mom they had, and that I didn't get to make the decisions. I can't believe how I stood this, now."

Explains Volpe, "A narcissist will belittle you around a table by simply raising an eyebrow or clearing his throat, and the child in you, no matter your age or qualifications, will recoil. There's no cure for them but you can recover for yourself and learn about boundaries. When you can name what it is, it becomes real and you will think wow, how stupid I was to put up with this."

Says Wendy, "One day I decided to google 'husband belittles me in public' and up came domestic violence, and looking at the list I realised I ticked every box, especially manipulating my reality. By taking my arm up a flight of stairs saying he was worried I'd fall, as though I was decrepit, he was whittling away at my self-confidence. These were the times when I thought I must get out, but I can't without money which he had control of. He would question almost everything I paid for with his credit card – each food item. This again made me feel guilty each time I used it – to feed our family. But when he felt like it, he'd come home with a new motorbike – his rules."

Around this time, Wendy decided enough was enough and began therapy. "I started getting very clever. I'd follow him and try to catch him in affairs and demand to see bank statements. When he did sit with me and look at three months of statements, I noticed he was very nervous. I don't know what he thought I was going to do. There were a couple of question marks but I had no real proof. Eventually I thought, this thing is consuming my life – I've got to let go and try to be me.

"Then came the mind games, the gaslighting. We'd discuss something the one day, maybe that we would go somewhere, and then the next day he'd try and say that the conversation never happened. No problem, I decided to record every conversation, which of course horrified him. He lied continually, and eventually I decided to put a tracker under his car. When he came home at night and was busy showering, I'd go out to the garage, grab it and charge it ready for the next day. I soon caught him in places he wasn't supposed to be. I'd wanted to confirm I wasn't imagining things – that he was lying."

He realised Wendy was on to him and instead of things improving, the abuse simply escalated with Luke going so far as to hide her medication. Eventually, when Wendy made things as uncomfortable for him as she could and showed that she was no longer bowing to his demands, it was agreed that he'd spend weekends and a few nights a week at their weekend place. "This was when I was convinced he was having an affair. He'd come home for two nights and I would have moved the furniture, which made him really angry. I simply said, 'Please pack up the rest of your things and move out. You're away five nights, let's just make it seven.' Surprisingly, he was emotional about this.

"Later when I thought about things, I was disappointed that I'd let my daughters see a man treat a woman the way their father had treated me – belittling me in public and disciplining me. But these days I'm a different person and beginning to find joy in life. What a difference, from dreading hearing the garage opening in the evening to spending time with my dogs and books and going out into nature. The dogs give me unconditional love, and I can have all four on the bed with me while I read without anyone commenting."

Says Lutchman, "Women like Wendy are constantly on the alert for what's coming next. They will freeze when they hear their partners come home, even have panic attacks. It's hard not to get stuck in that situation, where you are literally immobilised."

"I've still got a long way to go and it's baby steps for now. I can't see myself in another relationship right now, but we'll see," concludes Wendy.

Tips from FAMSA on leaving an abusive relationship:

• Plan your exit strategy.
• Know what you have – property, finances, policies etc.
• Ensure you can you access all your documentation.
• Make sure you have a certified copy of your identity card or book, and give it to someone you trust.
• Make sure you have your own bank account.
• Set money aside as and when you can.
• Store a spare set of clothes with someone else.
• Make sure you can access a neighbour or friend if you need to in a hurry.
• Work out a way you can send a sign when you need help.
• Speak to a religious leader, such as a minister or pastor.
• Walk into one of FAMSA's offices for assistance. A list of their locations around South Africa is on their website at www.familylife.co.za.
• Prioritise your mental and physical well-being.
• Define boundaries – stop the abuser mistreating you any longer.
• Never blame yourself, as you're not the issue.
• Don't try and fix the abuser – they need professional help.
• Create a strong support system. Don't be frightened to speak up and ask for help.
• Allow time to heal once you are out of an abusive situation.

CHAPTER 5

Workplace bullying

"Corporate mental health issues cost around R40 billion annually. This is more than the total value of the social grants given out in South Africa. If we kept our workplace in good mental health, we could afford the social grants."

— *Professor Renata Schoeman*

SECTION 23 OF THE Constitution of South Africa states that "everyone has the right to fair labour practices" and Section 10 says that "everyone has inherent dignity and the right to have their dignity respected and protected". This means that every worker in the country has the right to be treated with dignity and respect at work, and no worker has to put up with harassment by employers. Yet, even with our robust constitution there is no guarantee this will happen. In this chapter we explore various stories of workplace bullying, with advice on just how to deal with these situations.

A bully is a bully is a bully. This is what I've come to work out after months of researching this topic in all its forms. One of the most cruel and hardest to live with is workplace bullying. Whilst you can walk away from many types of bullying, very often your livelihood and possibly your dependents rely on your salary.

You might think that it's only junior staff who get bullied, but after listening to the numerous stories recounted to me I found that managers and executives aren't immune to being bullied themselves. Women bosses were the topic of a number of interviews for this chapter – mostly in a negative context. Is this possibly because in our still-patriarchal society, women sometimes feel they need to be seen as aggressive as a way of competing with their male counterparts? This is known as queen bee syndrome, where a woman in a position of authority views or treats subordinates more critically if they are women and favours men when it comes to promotion.

The toxic workplace

Petty motives – Christal's story

There are new terms that have come into being to describe difficult work situations, such as the toxic workplace, the hostile work environment, and many more. For journalist Christal*, who I introduced in Chapter 1, what appeared to be a dream job come true turned into a nightmare. "I'd worked my way up to become a full features writer at the previous magazine I worked for, and this was the job I thought I was taking at the new magazine. Obviously I saw my path going upwards and forwards – not backwards and downwards, to start again as a junior writer. But every interaction I had from day one under my new editor got me down. The only type of articles she would give me to write would be small, unimportant pieces and even then she'd generally turn her nose up at my efforts. And when I say efforts, they were the very best I could do. She once made me rewrite an article four times, after screaming at me in our open-plan office like I was an imbecile.

"The thing was," continues Christal, "that being so young and inexperienced at life, I didn't question anything and, after all, this was my bread and butter." After several months of tolerating her boss's behaviour, Christal suddenly started to wonder just why her predecessor had left in what seemed to have been a rush. "I had her email address, so decided to ask her if it was just me that elicited such venom from this woman. She immediately replied that no, that's exactly what happened to her. In fact it turned out that she had experienced a bit of a breakdown, which was why she left. I still didn't know what to do but my partner at the time suggested I go to HR [human resources]. For me the point was that even if they said something to her, I would still have to work with her."

Eventually things became so bad for Christal that, with her nerves frayed, she became scared of handing in her work. "I'd get to the office really early and try and keep out of her way as much as I could. One day, as I reached the office, I found myself circling the block twice as I just couldn't bring myself to walk into the building and face her. I went to a fast-food place a block away, sat and called my mom in tears, telling her I couldn't go into the building. She told me not to worry, but to come home. No job was worth me working and worrying myself to death over. My mother knew I was a hard worker and that I gave everything I had to my work. This was hard for my mom, as we were brought up knowing we needed jobs.

"Other family members weren't surprised and said they had just been waiting for me to leave. The next day I resigned and then was working out my final month. They obviously hired a new person to take over from me, and for a week or two we were there together. At the last features meeting a couple of days before my final day I was told by my boss I had to attend the meeting, which I thought was strange, particularly as I could have been going to a competitor. The new features writer was of course also there. I was placed outside of the group around the table, on a chair in the corner. The poor new lady felt awkward but by now I was used to these games, meant to humiliate me, and instead I felt really amused by this. I knew exactly what my boss's motives were and now saw them for what they were – petty."

It wasn't to be the last time she'd hear from anyone in the company. "A couple of months after I left, the lady that had taken over from me called and asked if she could come and see me. When she arrived she poured out her story to me and there it was again – tales of abuse and bullying from the same woman. She felt as I did – that she was afraid to say anything to her colleagues and didn't really want to lose her job. This was obviously a serious pattern of abuse and until someone did something, nothing would change. Unfortunately, it's so often the whistle-blowers who get fired and because of this often battle to get another job. Today I can look back through a different lens, but at the time my anxiety around writing for magazines was so great I knew I couldn't go back into that world right then. The strange thing was that I could put words down on a page but I couldn't speak out."

Workplace fear

Like many of the interviews I conducted for this book, it was only when I assured people of complete anonymity that were they comfortable to speak to me about their workplace experiences. Unfortunately, explains Prof Schoeman, something many people like Christal have in common is the fear that if they speak up against bullying they'll be sidelined in their workplace. "People simply don't want to be the focus of this kind of attention. Bullying is hard to define as there are so many different grades. People don't always even realise they're being bullied. The overt type is name calling or shouting at someone – that's easy to spot as there are generally other people as witnesses. One thing is common with all bullying – it's always nasty. The quiet, more insidious type of bullying is the harder one to spot. This generally takes place when there's no one else around to witness the bad behaviour. If you're a high performer it can be worse, as you immediately think the problem must be on your side.

"Very often during a meeting, for instance where questions are being asked, you'll find yourself seemingly ignored, with someone else saying the same thing that's hailed as a great idea. Clearly, showing others that your opinion isn't valued is another way of bullying. This leads to someone internalising this situation and feeling they should try harder and work longer hours. They start doubting themselves. They won't speak up, because they now see themselves as the problem. The danger is when this leads to developing anxiety disorder, or even depression. If they're lucky enough to end up having therapy or treatment, someone will put this in the context of their experience and for the first time they can verbalise it as bullying – which they previously didn't recognise," explains Schoeman.

I also noticed that, during my interviews with the people in this chapter, the word "bullied" didn't always come into it. They knew they were getting a raw deal but didn't know how to verbalise this. Somehow, to say they were bullied seemed to them to show more vulnerability than they wanted to.

When asked whether women are indeed more likely to be bullied than men, Schoeman has a ready answer. "There are simply more women working for bosses than men in the workplace, so more women are on the receiving end, being bullied by both men and women," she explains.

"People don't know how to start when it comes to reporting what's happening to them. Very often human resources are just a punitive measure, or they're seen like that. They're not seen as people who are on your side or even sympathetic. They're there for the organisation more than the employees," says Schoeman.

These words about HR departments feature in almost every story here. I guess, if you look at the situation clearly, HR employees also work for the same bosses – the ones who pay your salary, pay theirs!

No check and balances – Thabi's story

This was exactly the case for Thabi*, whose first words to me were: "People think all the bullies are in the schoolyard, but make no mistake the corporate bullies are the same – they just act out in a different way.

119

With a playground bully, there's not the same power play or hierarchy involved and there's no livelihood attached to it." After 20 years of working in the world of insurance at the same company, Thabi could probably write her own book on bullying, but the instances that have stuck with her and changed her life are what she wants to share with me.

"In the corporate structure, I found that there are no checks and balances in place to counteract bullying. In all my years at this major organisation no one ever said, if there's bullying this is how you report it. So even if you do see bullying there's no route to follow it through. People are definitely afraid to come forward, which perpetuates the whole cycle. I decided early on I wasn't going to let anyone bully me – I was going to stand up for myself.

"We worked in teams and I had a great boss, but one day a new female team leader of another team asked me if I would go to a meeting with her and take minutes. This was something I could do easily, but I really hated taking minutes and certainly not for her, in another team. There was a new lady on her team who was inexperienced at taking minutes and she asked if I would help her. So we worked out that we would both take minutes, compare notes, and then I'd help her with the end product. What I never banked on was the insistency and rudeness of this other team leader, who wouldn't take no for an answer that I was the only person to do this. This became a big issue when I refused to type up these minutes, and I was called to a board meeting. I told them they could fire me, as when I started in this job I'd made it very clear that I don't type minutes. I said this woman was bullying me into doing something I didn't want to do. Even though she hadn't been with the company long, everyone knew she was a bully. From the time she started she felt she was better at her job than my boss, whose job she was in fact gunning for. The number of people she left in tears daily was incredible.

"My boss spoke up for me and no more was made of the incident. Although I was never asked to work for her again, our paths were still to cross. One day a colleague and I were walking in the corridor on our way to lunch, chatting normally. The next thing, her office door slammed so hard all the surrounding windows rattled. We jumped, and everyone from both sides of the corridor came running out to see what had happened. She had slammed the door; apparently she felt we were making noise – in her space. If she felt we were being noisy, all she had to do was stick her head out the door and say 'Hey guys, could you keep it down? I have a client with me', or something like that. But no, that wasn't her style. I went straight to my boss's office and told him what I felt. That someone in her position should be acting like that to people under her was simply wrong. Everyone else, it seemed, was scared to speak out for fear of her recrimination. Even though my boss spoke to her about the bullying, for the next few years it continued. In the end, people learnt how to deal with her and when she realised her bullying tactics were no longer working, she left."

Over the years, Thabi encountered many other cases of bullying. "One of the worst things that can happen is when you've come up through the company ranks with a colleague who then gets promoted, and their whole persona changes overnight. At the same time, this particular man started an affair with a lady he'd recommended for a post in his group. As I knew both him and his wife well, this put me in a very awkward spot, particularly when he made it clear that my work rating was at his discretion and if I didn't do things his way, this could easily drop. Other people also soon realised what was going on, particularly when she was promoted well above her pay grade. Suddenly this previously 'nice' man changed completely and became the office bully. The complaints ranged from his off-colour jokes to his only hiring people of his own ethnic background. This was when I realised complaining to HR was a waste of time, and eventually he was just moved to another division. The system failed the employees over and over again."

Understanding workplace bullying

As we know, bullying can apply to anyone from toddlers to octogenarians, but there are obvious differences in just how the bullying evolves as people get older. When you're small it's a sly pinch or an outright punch, but as we read in these stories as you get older the bullying is less physical and more insidious.

The subtlety of office bullying is what makes it stand apart from other types. According to Schoeman, "It can be labelling or name-calling. When someone is perhaps late one day and they're told 'you're always late'. Then you go one level further where you get deliberate bullying, or what I call the psychopath in the corridor. This is where people may simply withhold important information you need for your work until the last minute, or completely, and then expose you as though you're to blame. This could stop your work being approved or financially impact the company."

For Ragani*, chief people officer at a large corporate, her title says it all. Passionate about all things employee related, she sees human resources in a whole new light. "I will take the potential for development over value-add to business any day. It's time to take a different perspective on the way things have been done in human resources. It's hard to comment on other people and companies' stories, but I think it's all about taking a balanced approach but at the same time having absolutely zero tolerance when one human being belittles another. If someone is continually being mentioned as a bully, you shouldn't have to wait until they leave. They should at least be looked into and action taken, whether it's counselling or something else."

As I listened to these experts in the field of workplace bullying, I also realised what a difficult position they are generally placed in, as, like educator Paul Channon commentated on school children, it's often a case of whose side do you believe? One party feels righteous and the other wronged.

From an HR point of view, identifying and dealing with bullying is no straightforward matter. Companies generally like issues to disappear quietly without causing a stir, explains Dr Ruwayne Kock, an organisational psychologist and global people management specialist with 25 years of experience locally and internationally. "The problem will always exist of 'he said, she said', and sifting through the evidence to find the facts. Very often a bully's name will come up constantly over a period of time and that makes it easier for them to be identified."

Prof Schoeman endorses this view. "Occasionally you will get a situation where it may appear someone is bullying you, but part of their job is teaching you and unfortunately it can be perceived as 'they're shouting at me'. Very often strong people are also very prone to being rude. For the person they're teaching, this can then lead to self-doubt. The problem is that as soon as someone talks to HR about a possible bullying situation, they generally want to start an investigation, which leads to the 'he said, she said' scenario. Unless there are actual witnesses to the bullying who will come forward, how can it be proved? The bully's retort may simply be, 'I was just playing around – it wasn't serious.' And occasionally you'll find someone labelled as a bully who is just someone who doesn't have good personal skills, and when addressed will simply back off. They're genuinely not aware of what they're doing."

At this point, let's remember that the definition of bullying is the act of intimidating a person perceived as vulnerable, and in a work situation, this is coupled to a formal power imbalance. Even when a workplace bully is confronted by their bosses, can they ever really change? One person I interviewed said that at a work leadership feedback session, when a colleague was told they were autocratic and controlling, they responded by saying, "That's just who I am." We've all met people like this. The difference is when you meet them in a social setting you can walk away without having to see them again – not so much in the workplace.

Adds Kock, "Very often bullies are easy to spot as their ego is what drives them to become a bully. Workplace bullying can, of course, be very subtle. For instance, you can arrive at a meeting with your team to find the boss has already made decisions without you, regarding your projects. But they're the boss and so – untouchable! Or are they?

"The sad thing is, people will often leave a company without saying anything about what happened to them. They just get to the point where they can't take any more and they can see that the company simply turns a blind eye to bullying. They feel their work goes unrecognised, and that they're taken for granted. It's not that people need constant praise but some recognition of good work should take place.

"When there are courses run for staff around leadership and issues such as bullying, the problem is the CEOs don't attend, when in fact they need this training desperately. Sadly, we live in a country with a culture of bullying – where society dictates. From a cultural point of view, very often people are scared to talk out," Kock comments.

The thin line: sexual harassment and culture in the workplace

If you ask anyone whether they spoke out about every wrongdoing they'd witnessed, you'd likely come out with a big fat zero. Why? Because as humans, we tend to naturally wait for someone else to speak up – we don't want to be "the one".

Very often, those who do choose to speak out end up paying the ultimate price – their jobs and their mental health. "It wasn't that I was scared of being bullied at work – after all, this wasn't my house, it was my job and they were paying my salary," explains news writer Lisa*. "I felt I could look after myself, but somehow I felt particularly responsible for the young girls working with me. When a female co-worker started becoming touchy-feely with me, I made it clear that this wasn't for me. She didn't try anything again, but she did become vindictive. Somehow I felt this contributed to making me a better journalist.

"Funnily enough, a few years later a similar incident occurred. The media industry in South Africa being quite small means that reputations are easily gained and not easily lost, so when I went to work at another radio station and saw a particular guy working there, I expected trouble. He had a reputation for cornering young women and trying it on. He would particularly do this with young interns, who before long came to me to tell me he would do things like touch their legs when they were in the middle of an interview, which naturally made them feel very uncomfortable. Although he didn't try this with me, I took the role of superhero and confronted him, saying that some of the girls told me they felt uncomfortable, and let's sort this out so we can just carry on with our jobs. He immediately got up from his desk and went into the newsroom, where two staff and an intern were sitting, and said, 'Lisa said I'm making the young women feel uncomfortable – is that true?' They said, 'Dude, no.' I resigned soon after that, as he became very spiteful towards me."

Dealing with sexual harassment issues in the workplace is very complex, as the line between what is seen as sexual harassment, versus a compliment or friendly banter, is blurred. When I was working in the United States I quickly became aware of a very different atmosphere and awareness around such issues in my workplaces. My male colleagues told me how they had to be super careful not to say or do anything to a colleague that could be construed as sexual harassment. One guy told me how a random remark made in a lift about being squeezed together like sardines could be made to sound bad. He knew this from personal experience.

"Education on what is actually sexual harassment is vital in an organisation," explains Kock. "What might be seen as a joke to one person could be highly offensive to another. Education reinforced with policy should be part of a company's values. What does work is to create 'allies', for instance men who, when sitting in a group and someone says something inappropriate, will say 'it's not correct to say that'. You need to have these allies for support in racial or sexual situations.

"You also shouldn't keep quiet but talk to someone in the company you trust, whether it's an HR person or a counsellor, or just a colleague. Intuitively you know it's wrong, but sometimes you think, is it just me? But when it happens a second or third time – it's not you. Don't be silent. Check with others if they've had similar experiences with a particular person, then start creating detailed notes with times, dates and situations, so when this is exposed you've got detailed information. It's a tough situation and you need a solid support structure around you."

This view is endorsed by Ragani: "There are no real textbook answers when it comes to dealing with such issues. We hold workshops for staff so they are fully aware of what their rights are, whether this is within their area of work or perhaps sexual harassment. The bottom line is that you need a cohesive work environment where everyone feels valued and listened to. It shouldn't be them and us."

"Blatant" – Jody's story

The problem in specialist fields such as broadcast news is that the job market is tight, and people don't always have the luxury of walking out the door. Standing up to racial inequality or hatred, gender inequality or bullying is often seen as something beyond reach if you want to keep your job.

"Choice is a luxury of the rich," explains Jody*. "The owner and founder of a small company I worked for was nothing less than a gross human being. How else do you describe a blatantly racist, ignorant, hateful individual? In a meeting one day he turned to a black colleague and asked, 'How many languages do you speak?' To which the guy replied, 'English.' The boss's obviously snide retort was, 'Surely you speak other things at home?' How do you answer this, when you're a young black guy talking to an elderly white man who's your boss?"

"Things became so bad at this company that a group of us, after contacting former employees who had the same issues as us, considered taking out a court case against him," says Jody. "I went to try and speak to the HR manager, who instead of listening became very irate. After this the situation became very intense. The boss knew I had complained about him and although he never said anything, I was aware HR had told him. It became a case of how much I needed the job, against putting up with this kind of working environment. I chose my health in the end, and actually think the whole ordeal made me a stronger person.

"It still doesn't make sense to me why HR departments and companies don't do better with bullying and abuse. Surely the main goal is to look after the business's interests, which means having a cohesive, happy workforce. You are paying people to do what you hope will be the best work they can produce for you. When they're not being heard and are unhappy in their work environment, this isn't going to happen," emphasises Jody.

The role of human resources

There's a definite link between being bullied and abused, particularly in the workplace, explains Prof Schoeman. "This, again, is where HR should come in to determine this. But as I've said, their role is mostly punitive and they often don't appear to be on the employees' side or show any sympathy for their situation."

Dr Kock notes, "It often stems from an intolerance to differences but over the last few years quite a lot of work has been done around tolerance, equity and inclusion in the workplace. It's about making sure everyone feels included and treated equally. HR departments should be creating workplaces that are psychologically safe, and that those in charge are the right people to ensure these values."

The cold shoulder – Stuart's story

Echoing Jody's experience and feelings around HR departments is Stuart[*], who after working in a senior corporate IT position for over 50 years, felt he was valued by his company. This was not just for his high-level IT skills but also for his particular business sector knowledge. His work entailed heading up major projects for his company and all was going well until he found he needed urgent orthopaedic surgery for a shoulder disorder. I could tell it was hard for Stuart to talk about his experience, which has definitely had a major impact on his life.

"I begged the surgeon to postpone the operation until the project was finished, but he left me in no doubt of the urgency if I didn't want to end up permanently disabled.

"In the next month, although I was in severe pain, I put what I thought was everything in place and did a complete handover for my absence over my three weeks' sick leave. The surgery was successful and I went home to recuperate. Eight days later, my boss called to say they were desperate and could I join them for an online meeting. During the meeting, rather than being in a consultancy role, I found I was being handed work to do. I mentioned that I wasn't comfortable with this but was simply told, it's really urgent and I had no choice. When the meeting was over, I contacted our HR representative and told her I was really battling with this as I was on sick leave and felt this wasn't okay. Very quickly I received a call from my boss, asking why I'd escalated this to HR. I told him that no one would listen when I said I was off work recovering from a serious operation, and that I didn't think I should be given work to do during this time.

"After this I was left alone, but when I eventually got back to work I found I was excluded from all the projects I'd been working on. I asked a colleague why I'd now been left out of these projects, and was told it was because I'd left my original project in a terrible state and had lied to them about how advanced things were. He actually went on and on justifying their actions, while I was completely flummoxed because I genuinely felt I was being treated very unfairly.

"To make things even worse, on the night of my first day back I was called and told I had to do work that night, outside of working hours, to sort out an urgent issue. I knew there were other people who could do this. When I approached colleagues about the situation, I was told in no uncertain terms that the problem was me. It didn't take long to work out that the colleague who'd been responsible for doing my work when I was on sick leave had put the blame firmly on me when the project started to go wrong. This hurt even more, as we had become personal friends as well as colleagues.

"I was used to working nights and weekends – it had been part of the job, which as a senior person in the company meant no overtime. I loved my job and hadn't minded this, but when I was in a neck brace and still feeling physically uncomfortable, this just wasn't right. When I pointed out that my contract clearly states my work hours as eight and a half hours a day and that I was on beck and call 24 hours a day, that didn't even get a response. I did get a vague apology for being bothered whilst on sick leave and on my first day back, but this was far from sincere. Over time I saw things were never going to go back to normal and with no one to turn to, as HR were certainly not on my side, in anger and pain I resigned. I realised shortly after, given my age, that this was a rash decision particularly during the Covid-19 lockdown – but I'd been at a low point, really upset and emotional.

"After checking out the job market I realised this hadn't been a well thought-out decision and I ended up grovelling to my boss to get my job back. I had to write a seriously humiliating letter begging to let me withdraw my resignation. After telling me I could come back, I was told I would receive no increase or bonus that year, had a written warning, and that I'd have to write a document explaining how I'd work with my colleague professionally going forward. What could I do? I was stuck between a rock and a corporate hard place," explains a frustrated Stuart.

"It's been a tremendous growth experience for me. I've since had to go through some intense therapy with a psychologist, but have turned things around at work and hit the top appraisal rung this year. I hated humiliating myself and it was a difficult place to come back from. My colleague did eventually apologise but our relationship will never be the same. As for HR, when push comes to shove they answer to the company and aren't going to stand up for you. They're an enforcement weapon if you step out of line – you'll be fired.

"There was no appeal structure – no one to listen to you. All this hidden under a banner of protocol, where they're allowed to treat you like this. I've since seen other colleagues bullied in a similar manner but now keep my thoughts to myself. I also learnt a lot about workplace politics and do all I can to stay well away from this. It's definitely dog-eat-dog in the corporate world – a constant power play, with people scrambling over each other to get to the top. They almost encourage this culture of fear, with the only option being if you want to leave – then go," Stuart concludes.

Dr Kock is only too aware of such situations: "HR should be the avenue for people to report and get their issues listened to. They should be the place to go to talk about difficult situations, whatever type of bullying someone experiences. Some companies have 'employee champions' who are there to represent the employees. This would be the person who would be the one in a meeting to say, 'What does this mean from an employee perspective? What does it mean for our well-being?'

"Some large organisations have ombudsmen working independently of the HR department, where people can raise issues more anonymously. But even with this, there are pros and cons. The difficulty sometimes is that these people see their role as independent of HR, as not integrating what they're doing with the internal processes of the organisation. If you're going to have an ombudsman, then they still have to work within the company guidelines."

Stuart talked about an appeal process, which Kock says should be available in these situations. "It depends on whether an initial hearing is held or not. This is where having an independent ombudsman can be of use, as long as it fits into the company's legislative procedure. People are usually notified beforehand of a hearing, which should have an independent chairperson overseeing it, but this doesn't mean it won't possibly be biased or even predetermined. Most organisations are pretty good at keeping independence here. As a last resort, you can take your case to the CCMA [Commission for Conciliation, Mediation and Arbitration] or even the Labour Court. You shouldn't be victimised by doing this, but there is a possibility this would be the case."

The Devil wears Prada – Cindy's story

In all the similar workplace stories I heard, none were as horrendous as Cindy's* when it came to being taken advantage of, whilst being constantly intimidated by toxic organisational culture. She worked for the ultimate boss-zilla at a small but powerful company in its field. I'd heard about this boss from several people but was still not prepared for the story Cindy related.

"I started there in the capacity of executive assistant and when I initially enquired just how much personal stuff I'd have to do, I was told 'as and when required'. That, simply put, isn't a job description but a licence for abuse – or at least it was in my case."

Naturally, when you first meet your boss they're generally on best behaviour. After all, who would take a job if they suspected they were about to work for a narcissistic, half-deranged person? But it didn't take Cindy long before she realised just what she'd gotten herself into. "It was almost impossible for my boss not to show her true colours, frequently shouting and screaming at everyone. Mind you, that depended whether you were on her current 'cool kids' list or not. If you were 'in' that month you could get away relatively unscathed, but should you be on her 'shit list' things were different."

Apart from doing her normal administrative duties Cindy was expected to wear several hats, including au pair to boss-zilla's six-year-old child (also in training to be a boss-zilla) and her mother, who obviously had the genetic make-up that produced boss-zilla. "The first calls generally started at around 7 am, where to get a repairman for something at the house, to take her mother to hospital or child to school, and so on. I get that as an executive assistant you would be expected to go the extra mile, but I wasn't expecting an ultra-marathon. I also didn't know this was a seven-days-a-week job and one where the word 'thanks' or even 'please' never played a role."

Cindy almost didn't know where to start telling me of her Machiavellian boss's habits, but perhaps one thing stood out in particular. After Cindy had been there for a few months and got to know her colleagues, she realised most of them had one thing in common – they were all without partners or children to weigh them down, leaving more time to throw themselves into work. This was no accident and was a factor in choosing staff. "I also got to know her incredibly devious ways of playing one of us against the other. She would say, 'So Cindy, what do you think of...' and then go to them and ask the same about me or someone else. I realised this was part of her insecurity. So as brash as she was, she was also highly insecure, always seeking affirmation from those around her. And she would get it, as they were all vying to be in her good books.

"As for complaining to HR about anything, this was impossible as the woman running HR had been a former PA of hers, who boss-zilla informed me she'd instructed to be her 'ears and eyes' in the company.

"Perhaps the worst moments were when she would dress you down by screaming at you in front of other people – staff and clients. When I later told her I didn't appreciate being yelled at like that in front of other people (although that was common in our offices) her reply would be, 'Okay, noted' and of course nothing would change."

You're probably reading this thinking, why didn't Cindy just leave? As a 54-year-old woman she was scared she wouldn't find another reasonably paid, interesting job. Added to which her confidence was slowly being eroded by her narcissistic boss. "My friends and family thought I was crazy to stay. I'd be at their homes at night or on a weekend when the dreaded name would pop up on my phone. 'Not again!' they'd say, and I had to shrug and get on with it."

Although lockdown during Covid did mean she could work from home, Cindy's life didn't become any easier. "Here was this woman who ran a highly successful business, but who didn't even own a laptop and certainly didn't embrace the digital world. During lockdown I would have to download her emails, print them out and then send them to her in an Uber. She was neurotic about being near anyone, which suited me at the time. What businesswoman in her forties can run a business like that?

"Even though I didn't see her each day, the flood of requests never stopped. I'd get regular shopping lists, including big items like beds and household furnishings, which I'd have to pay for with my personal credit card and then wait until the end of the month to be reimbursed!"

But the turning point for Cindy came when she heard that boss-zilla was planning a move to another province to operate from her branch there. At first Cindy thought this might be a good change for her, as she also had family there and liked the town. But as time went by and nothing was mentioned about her going along, she began to realise that she was perhaps not part of the move. "This, along with worsening abuse, made me realise I had to look for another job, which surprisingly, I got really quickly. What was so apparent during the four-interview process was the professionalism of this other company, and I knew I wouldn't find any workplace abuse there."

It gave Cindy great pleasure to send an email with her resignation. "I didn't feel she even deserved a telephone call so I sent her a mail and her response was quick, asking 'WHAT ARE YOU THINKING?' – in capitals of course, followed by a large number of exclamation marks. When I told her that as I hadn't heard about moving with her, I felt I needed to make other plans, she said of course I would be going with – after all, I was part of the family! What a joke. All the times she'd asked, no ordered me, telling me she NEEDED food for her and her family or NEEDED a cappuccino, she never once asked if I would like anything for myself. I wouldn't treat anyone like that, let alone a family member. After I resigned she also offered me R20 000 more than I'd been getting – an amount I should have received all along. That made me even more certain I was making the right move."

And it wasn't just Cindy who didn't stick around at the company, although she was one of the longer-term employees. "The average turnover of staff in this company of around 30 staff members was six or eight members a year. Boss-zilla never looked inwards when this happened but always had a reason to justify their leaving. The best day should have been my last day, but this was not to be as she kept begging me to just stay another week. Luckily my new company were very kind and allowed me to do this, but there came a point where I said no more, I'm out of here – and I've never looked back. These days I wake up with a lightness I'd forgotten I could have and wish I'd left far sooner. When I think back I can't believe this was my life – but for six years it was a living hell."

Cindy's situation, according to Kock, is a definite case of a lack of leadership and developing a healthy company culture in the way things are done. "In companies like this, very often you'll find their culture is the same as it's been for years. As long as the staff create results, that's all that counts. They may produce – but at what expense to the morale and health of the staff? Such situations aren't sustainable over long periods of time. Staff burn out quickly and the annual turnover of staff is high. I often get called in to see why this is happening, and frequently what I find is that the leadership are the toxic ones."

Ragani adds, "Although many companies say they have an open-door policy, very few staff are comfortable walking through that door. It's not enough to tell your staff this is available to them, they need to be assured that someone will really listen to them and advise them on what to do next.

"It comes down to having the right systems in place and that the staff know how to use them. Companies must be prepared to listen and make sure that each member of staff is heard and, where necessary, action is taken," concludes Ragani.

What does the law say?

The Employment Equity Act 55 of 1998 states in clause 6 (1) that: "No person may unfairly discriminate, directly or indirectly, against an employee, in any employment policy or practice, on one or more grounds, including race, gender, sex, pregnancy, marital status, family responsibility, ethnic or social origin, colour, sexual orientation, age, disability, religion, HIV status, conscience, belief, political opinion, culture, language and birth."

And although South African labour law doesn't specifically define what workplace harassment is in terms of this act, the Commission for Conciliation, Mediation and Arbitration (CCMA) has developed information sheets that confirm that harassment in the workplace includes:

- *Sexual harassment* – unwanted and unwelcome conduct of a sexual nature that is physical, verbal or non-verbal, that includes touching, kissing, rape, strip-searching, following or watching, threats, innuendo, unwelcome gestures and sexual favouritism.

- *Racial, ethnic or social origin harassment* – this includes but is not limited to racist verbal and non-verbal conduct, racially offensive written or visual material, open hostility, subtle or blatant exclusion from workplace activities and threatening behaviour.

- *Bullying* – the CCMA considers the following, amongst others, to be classed as examples of bullying:
  - spreading malicious rumours;
  - insulting persons;
  - degrading, or picking on, another;
  - exclusion or victimisation;
  - unfair treatment;
  - overbearing supervision;

- unwelcome sexual advances and/or gestures;
- making unsubstantiated threats about job security;
- undermining a competent worker by means of overloading or constant criticism;
- intentional blocking of promotion or training opportunities.[16]

The CCMA says that workplace bullying may be physical, emotional or verbal harassment. The Commission goes on to advise that a worker should take notes and keep a record of every instance of alleged bullying. This is so that there is proof of the allegations.

The CCMA also says the person being harassed should confront the harasser directly, where reasonable, to stop the harassment – but to be sure to have a witness present. If the bullying behaviour doesn't stop, the worker should lodge a grievance under the company's grievance policy. Once the case has been reported, the employer is obliged to investigate the case and, if necessary, disciplinary action must be taken against the harasser.

Tips for dealing with workplace bullying:

What can I do?
Don't be embarrassed to tell people what's happening so you can get help. You might find others are going through the same thing.

Get advice
Find out the best route you can take to seek help, possibly from:
• An employee representative, such as a trade union official.
• Someone in the company's human resources department.
• Your manager or supervisor.

Stay calm
Try and understand that criticism or personal comments have nothing to do with your abilities. They reflect the bully's own weaknesses, meant to intimidate and control you.

Talk to the bully
As hard as it may be, try and talk to the bully and let them know how their behaviour is affecting you. Try to stay calm and be polite. If you feel you're not up to this, then you could get someone else to do this for you.

Keep a diary
As mentioned above, this is really important for when you do take action.

Make a formal complaint
Find out just what your employer's grievance procedure is and follow the suggested route.

What about legal action?
After this, if nothing changes you may have to look at taking legal action, which may mean contacting the CCMA. Get professional advice before you do this.

Adapted from the National Health Service (UK).[17]

CHAPTER 6

Cyberbullying

ACCORDING TO We Are Social and Hootsuite's recent study, the *Digital 2022 Global Overview Report*,[18] South Africa has the most addicted internet users in the world, spending an average of 10 hours and 46 minutes a day online. Of this time, 35 per cent (2 hours and 27 minutes on average per day) is spent on social networks. This was taken from the 16–64-year-old age group, but in my research some of the most addicted users of this medium were under the age of 16. And according to a survey conducted by Digimune of South African parents to gauge their views and concerns around children and digital threats, it emerged that over 51 per cent of children had been cyberbullied, and 54 per cent of children had accessed inappropriate content via digital platforms.[19]

So with cyberbullying being so rife today, I was surprised at the reaction my requests for interviews around this topic received. Appealing through colleagues, mental health professionals, schools, social media and more, I was receiving similar feedback – cyberbullying exists and it's dreadful, but none of the victims want to talk about it. At first I didn't quite understand this, but after more research I realised the pain and anguish cyberbullying can inflict on someone, particularly a young person with limited life experience. So the approach, it seemed, was that it was far better to try and put the bullying out of your mind – which would be made harder by retelling and reliving those dreadful emotions, not to mention the embarrassment attached to becoming involved in such incidents.

Bullies without names or faces

Those I was able to speak to, and whose stories are retold below, were brave enough to share these dreadful encounters with me. Or perhaps I shouldn't call them encounters, as a large part of the problem with cyberbullying is that your assailants are faceless...

I also spoke to those on the other side, who admitted they didn't realise what damage their tweets or posts would do to those on the receiving end. They wished they could take them back, but that's the thing with the internet – once out there, you lose control of your words and images, and they can be copied and replicated without permission or any time limits. That in itself is a warning to think before you post, forward or repost.

We're living in a social media whirl of seeing who can become a serious influencer, get the most followers, likes, shares, heart emojis, and hopefully sponsors knocking on the door to do deals. Addiction these days doesn't necessarily have anything to do with alcohol or drugs – it's more likely to refer to the number of hours people spend glued to their phones or devices, watching endless hours of TikTok or going from one social media app to the next. Mental health professionals are seeing more and more of this phenomenon, which is fast becoming a serious and difficult addiction to break.

According to Cayley Jorgensen, there's no way to describe the popularity and addictiveness of platforms such as Instagram, TikTok, Snapchat, Twitter and others. "This has led to even more openings for bullying than ever. There are even confession pages, where you can post anonymous words about anybody on the page. This of course leads to a lot of mocking and bullying from which the spinoffs are a disaster, especially for a young person's mental well-being."

The results of this fascination and the power that social media has over people is the rise in mental health issues, often leading to people taking their own lives. Once exposed in any way on social media these people, often very young, don't seem to be able to shrug off the massive dark cloud someone else's words about them has cast. The only way out for them is a final one.

Proof of this is evident on a regular basis in the media with headlines such as: "Girl, 13, commits suicide after allegedly being bullied on WhatsApp", after a photograph was sent around her school via the messaging platform.[20]

The photo, it seems, had gone viral over the previous week and she saw suicide as the only option to counter the shame. She was afraid to go to school on the Monday after the incident started, and her mother met with the school principal that morning. When the mother returned home, she found her daughter's lifeless body.

Sextortion

A global issue, it's not just South Africa that sees such incidents. Last year a 17-year-old American in his final year of school in Michigan fell prey to a social media blackmailer. What he saw on Instagram was a pretty girl who messaged him asking to exchange intimate images. At first he was sceptical but when he received a photo from her, he decided to take a chance. He should have stuck with his initial gut feeling, because shortly after the "pretty girl" received the photo, a demand of $1 000 was made with the threat that unless he paid up, the image he sent would go to all his online friends. Not having the $1 000 demanded he sent $300 instead, which the blackmailer wasn't happy with. The teen, now terrified, replied, "You win, I'm going to kill myself." The blackmailer responded, "Go ahead."[21] Within hours, this young man with his whole life ahead of him was dead by his own hand. A victim of what has come to be known as **sextortion**.

> **Sextortion:** a fairly new word, defined by the *Cambridge Dictionary* as "the practice of forcing someone to do something, particularly to perform sexual acts, by threatening to publish naked pictures of them or sexual information about them: a crime of the digital age."[22]

I witnessed the fear of this racket first-hand when a colleague of mine was targeted by a scam that was going around a lot in 2020. We were at the airport waiting to catch a flight, both going through our emails and social media when they looked up to me in horror with fear written all over their face. When I asked what was going on, they sheepishly showed me their phone. They had received an anonymous SMS telling them that, unless they paid over 10 000 bitcoin in the following 24 hours, all the porn pages they'd downloaded would be revealed to all their social media contacts. Luckily I had seen an exposé on this very topic on *Carte Blanche* a week or so before, so knew it was a scam. When I told them this, and that they should ignore it, I could still see the fear in their eyes. It was only a few days later when nothing had happened that they relaxed, realising how they were nearly relieved of a good deal of money.

Cyber stranger danger

For Dean McCoubrey, founder of MySocialLife, an organisation set up to help learners and schools navigate the challenges of today's technology and social media, these are not unusual stories. "We were told by our parents never to speak to strangers or go home with them, but the difference here is that kids can't see who they're online with. They are similar scenarios, but with the online situation parents feel lost, as they don't understand the platforms their children are on. Very often it's a case of having their heads in the sand, and we need to gently pull those heads out and create awareness.

"I had a father call me while his son was being sextorted by an Indian crime ring. He'd heard me talking on the radio and desperately needed help – literally that instant. They'd contacted his son posing as a girl and asking him to expose himself, which he did. Now they were on the phone demanding money, otherwise they'd go viral to all his contacts. We were able to take control of this situation, but generally people panic and give these people what they want – money.

"These are the stories that no one wants to talk about, but we know they're happening on a daily basis worldwide. Where there's money to be made, the scamsters are on full alert, targeting not just naïve youngsters but people of all ages, with a common link – a fear of being exposed as vulnerable, stupid or, worse, as perverts or sluts to their peers."

A common thread I found throughout my research was that when an adult or child feels they're complying with someone online, that: a) they're acting anonymously; and b) if they don't do it, they're not cool. Neither is true.

According to clinical psychologist Liane Lurie, sexual bullying is firmly on the increase. "What people don't realise is that this starts from the age of 12 and younger, where we see kids sending nude photos of themselves, particularly girls to boys. If they don't, boys pressure them, while other girls think 'it's cool'. With apps like WhatsApp and now the very popular TikTok, the growth of this behaviour is staggering. For kids, the fact that their parents are generally not present in their online environment makes this a lot easier."

For Jorgensen, looking at this situation from a developmental perspective, it's a tricky issue to deal with. "Teens are still very much in an impulsive state. If someone asks for something, they think, 'I need to do this right now'. Their brains are still developing in terms of understanding consequences and long-term ramifications. After a girl has been bullied to where she sends a nude photo of herself, she will say to me afterwards, 'I know I shouldn't have done it. I didn't want to do it, but I did...'

"A lot of girls, in particular, are feeling pressurised from judgement at school and want to feel accepted; so if I send a nude then this guy is really going to like me, and if someone else likes me I'm 'worth it'. It's similar to joining their peers to drink or smoke," Jorgensen adds.

"We try to teach them to look at such situations as what you *are* in control of, and what you're *not* in control of. Also, to understand that they are leaving a digital footprint online that won't go away."

A different world

In early 2022, Alison Gray, deputy principal of Westerford High School, granted me a singular opportunity: to spend time with a group of their students, between the ages of 13 and 17, who volunteered to speak freely to me about their feelings and experiences of social media and the pressures it brings. One 16-year-old young man freely admitted to having posted "mean things" about one of his peers to a friend, who, without his knowledge, reposted this on with dire consequences. "Before I even realised what had happened this post had spread like wildfire, and it didn't take long before I was the one receiving hate mail and messages telling me to kill myself. I immediately realised that what I'd written was really wrong and stupid, and even though I tried to fix it, it was way too late. It was one thing saying something hateful online, but quite another when you see what other people can do with that.

"At school I was completely ostracised by my group of friends and it was a really difficult time for me. But I realised that I'd done this to myself, and that there was no such thing as just sending a stupid message without thinking about it first. About the damage and harm you could do with your words."

A 16-year-old girl, particularly wise for her age, commented on how important it was that parents should be educated before their child is allowed on social media apps. This was a constant theme throughout my research on this chapter.

Another 14-year-old girl described how one of her best friends called her after she had been attacked for sticking up for someone else on social media. Once again, the phrase "you should just kill yourself" was bandied about, which seems to be a trend all on its own in these situations. "By the time she called me she was in a bad way, and said she thinks maybe she should kill herself. I was speechless and didn't really know what to do, but knew I had to keep her talking and try and convince her not to do this. When we stopped talking I felt she had calmed down but I couldn't stop thinking, what if she did something? And although I promised her I wouldn't, I told my parents. Even they didn't know how to solve this but they did get hold of her parents, who in turn contacted the school. The next day at school the situation had calmed down and those involved were censured." But, you could ask, what would have happened if this girl *had* taken her own life, which we know does happen – and what punishments fit such an incident?

According to this group of students, punishment over this type of bullying is very unclear. There is suspension or even expulsion from school, but the process is far from perfect right now. As many of them suggested, education and counselling would be better for the culprits. "No one really knows what to do in these circumstances but surely if we were taught how dangerous words and photos can be, and what it can do to the person involved, this would be more useful than suspending someone? Just suspending them, especially if they're a bully anyway, won't stop them doing it again," said the 14-year-old girl.

These young people had volunteered to talk to me, but I noticed one rather shy girl who was almost reluctant to talk in front of the others, and when she did it was with her head not quite up. She eventually spoke, saying, "When one of your friends texts mean stuff about another person, it's really hard not to agree with that. I don't want to ruin the friendship, so in most cases I just go along with it as I want to appear cool. It's much easier to agree than disagree..." After speaking her head dropped down again, looking at the desk rather than up at me.

I knew she realised what she had said was wrong, but also massively feared being thought of as not being cool.

Another rather mature-sounding student of 16 told the story of how an older friend of hers, who used to "randomly accept anyone on her Instagram account", ended up with a situation she could never have foreseen. "Using her photo, someone created a fake Instagram profile, swapping her head for that of a pig and an elephant, saying she should lose weight and that no one could love her. They also said she should kill herself and more. She phoned me sobbing, and although I didn't really know what to do I just kept her on the line, talking until I heard her fall asleep. She felt better the next day and started speaking about it, as well as deleting her Instagram account."

It's hard to listen to these young people, who seem to accept online harassment and startling hatred as almost normal. One 15-year-old summed it up perfectly: "I like to sing and perform, and my friends video this and I post it. What will people comment on? Not that they liked the music, but rather that I missed a note or my voice cracked at one point. People love to point out all the faults but I know that by putting myself out there, I can expect that."

I also asked this group what age they thought it was acceptable for children to be on social media and the consensus clearly was that, although they thought this should be from age 13, they also felt children and parents should be educated around the issues first. One said, "Before you even go on any social media, there should be a lot of educating from parents. There needs to be conversation around cyberbullying and situations around paedophiles and clicking on unknown links. Obviously parents would need to be educated themselves around these things to be able to make it safe for their kids."

Before you start judging parents, think of the immense pressure of knowing what your children are up to 24 hours a day. They're in their room doing homework or playing soccer, or hockey, or at swimming practice... But during all these times, they can just as easily be on their electronic devices.

"It's really very addictive," admitted one of the matric boys in the group. "You know it's there on your phone and sometimes I literally tell myself no, I need to focus on my school work or my family. I have thoughts of temporarily deleting or even disabling my accounts, but then I think, just let me check one more time, just for five minutes. Three hours later I'm still on it!

"There's always someone sexting, showing photos of people you know. We're told if someone sends you this, don't answer, just turn your phone off. Which is all very well, but what about when you come face to face with the person in the photo the next day? What do you do, what do you say in this situation? And if they don't know, it's even worse. So far I haven't been given any advice on what to do in that situation, whether it's happening to you or someone else."

One of the other matric girls in the group is nodding firmly as her fellow student speaks. "I think the worst part is when a minor is exposed to adult images and porn. When something like this happens parents aren't educated enough to decipher who's the victim here. Who's provoking this? This leads to a child feeling they're the victim when they're not. Parents need to learn about this – they're our guardians and we don't know how to handle it."

"Adolescents' brains are still developing and they're prone to impulsive behaviour," explains Jorgensen. "They don't realise the consequences of sending these images to someone. You may delete it on your side, and they may promise to delete it on theirs, but you don't know that same image is being sent to 10 others, that become 20, that become 100 and more. They don't realise that even if something is deleted, there's always going to be a permanent record out there.

"What's the highest form of validation for a developing girl? Sexual validation. And when they post pictures of themselves posing in suggestive photos, they don't realise these platforms are frequented by older men, although in the case of certain girls that is even stronger validation. For them it's often about how many likes and shares they're getting."

There are so many layers to adolescents, in particular, and social media. Simply seeing others who they perceive as having the perfect body, which goes with their perfect glamorous online life, is adding massively to the already high occurrence of eating disorders. "So many young people follow these accounts and do self-comparisons, followed by googling how to lose weight and even how to starve yourself thin," adds Jorgensen.

Social media is relentless, and we're only seeing the tip of the iceberg right now, Lurie feels. When you already have teen hormones raging out of control and then add social media bullying, a parent's life is made even harder. "Teens need to know who they are in today's world. They want their parents to be proud of them, to think of them in a certain way, and suddenly you're faced with this massive shame that you don't want anyone to know about. Even though parents assure their kids they can talk to them about anything, for the teen it's the most heart-wrenching, inconceivable thing to share."

Self-confidence is fragile – Romy's story

A social media incident doesn't even have to be as serious as sexting or sextortion to have a profound effect on someone's life. For Romy*, what should have been an insignificant incident turned into malicious and cruel behaviour from her peers at school. During one of the outbreaks of Covid-19, a fellow learner tested positive for the virus and naturally the school policy was for them to stay home. Romy woke one morning with a bit of a sore throat. It was a Friday and her mother, observing the school protocol, took Romy for testing that same day. The test came back negative so on Monday morning, as usual, Romy arrived for school. Somehow, word was out on the school's social media network that Romy was sick and definitely had Covid! Not only was there immense physical hostility towards her, but a WhatsApp group worked overtime, calling her a stupid idiot no-brains, and proclaiming that she was going to infect everyone by arriving at school. To prove their point, learners posted photos of themselves wearing double masks, and whenever Romy came near, scurried as far away as they could.

Many people could have shrugged and even laughed this behaviour off, but for Romy it was devastating. She took her schoolwork and school friendships seriously, and having girls who she thought were her friends now belittling her was too much. The next day she arrived at school with proof of her negative test, which was backed up by the school. To enforce their point, the school also closed down these girls' WhatsApp group. The old saying "the pen is mightier than the sword" played its role here, as it turned out social media was mightier than the school realised and other groups quickly sprang up.

Romy was lucky to have a mother she felt comfortable confiding in, and with her mom's help and reinforcement got through it and become even stronger in the wake of the incident.

Romy's mother Karen* explained to me that she had always made a point of stressing to Romy that there was nothing she couldn't tell her. That she wouldn't judge Romy, but would try and guide her in the right direction – and she'd always kept that promise. "Even Romy's friends feel they can talk to me, which is sometimes difficult as I have to promise them I won't tell their parents. I guess if I felt they were likely to be in any danger or seriously harm themselves, then I'd break that promise. With Romy, I only have to look at her walk through the door to know when something's wrong, and it doesn't take long before she tells me about it. I think the best thing about our relationship is that she never has to feel she's alone in these situations. She knows that between us, we can take care of anything."

What parents need to understand is that what may seem like a trivial incident to them, can feel enormous to a developing adolescent. Again, one of the biggest issues here is that parents feel the schools need to educate learners, and schools feel the responsibility lies firmly with the parents. A no-win situation.

Schools ignoring cyberbullying

"With cyberbullying a huge issue right now, getting buy in from teachers and schools to use outside help for this type of education should be a priority," explains Jorgensen. "The problem with many schools, however, is that by seeking such help, this is announcing the school has problems – which they don't want to admit. There's no school that's immune to this situation, and the sooner they start educating and supporting their learners the better.

"The main issues we're seeing with cyberbullying are exclusion, reputation damage and, of course, gossiping. With boys, it's different. Here it often happens on gaming platforms where boys talk to their peers playing the game, many of whom they often don't know, but the messages are generally more direct than with girls. They'll call each other names if they think someone is messing up in the game and will repost specific images, which of course can cause massive harm, particularly in a world of fast-growing child sexual exploitation."

The sooner schools wake up and smell the cyber roses, the sooner they will be able to inform their students and parent body of the dangers out there.

For Alison Gray, the last 20 years have seen major changes in students' social media usage. "When I first started at the school cell phones were completely banned between 8 am and 3 pm, including breaks. If we found them, they were confiscated until the following Monday. Parents didn't like this at all at the time, but of course this was also before the days of social media and advanced technology.

"The school then introduced tablets, so trying to keep students off social media platforms became impossible. What we did see happening was that students were losing their social skills. No longer were they bursting out of class talking to their friends, but rather sitting and peering at their devices the second they got the chance. Even when they're sitting next to their friends they'd rather WhatsApp them than have a conversation, or check their Instagram to see how many likes they've received for a post.

"So we've introduced a middle road, where between 8 am and 3 pm, in corridors or classrooms, we don't want to see cell phones or earphones plugged in. Once they're let out at break times they can obviously use them, or if the teacher allows it for educational reasons.

"In terms of bullying, the Department of Basic Education does issue guidelines and we're currently working on a specific anti-bullying policy. What we do find is that students are scared to talk to their parents or teachers when these issues arise. The fear is to be labelled a snitch. We try to instil the importance of integrity in our learners, telling them that if they see something happening and do nothing, they're condoning it. Silence is condoning. We try and say to them we don't even need your name, we will keep that secret.

"What they don't realise is that if they send a screenshot of something, then the evidence is there and we don't need names. We urge them to find their voices, speak up for someone or yourself, go to a staff member you trust and say something. We do hear things from parents who also want to stay anonymous, but even so a lot goes unheard or unseen," concludes Gray.

The shaming starts early – Anna's story

This was exactly the situation for Anna*, now 19, when she first encountered cyberbullying at the age of 11. "A lot of my school friends were guys, so naturally I would post pictures of them on my Instagram account. What I didn't think of was the fact that other girls saw this as something completely different, and suddenly I'd see comments such as 'Oh, you're such a slut' or 'You shouldn't be friends with ___ because you know such and such a girl likes him'. At 11, it was incomprehensible for me that I could be labelled a slut for posting some photos of me with guys. These were also 11-year-old boys, after all."

Although she tries to hide it, I can hear the anger and hurt in Anna's voice just talking about these memories. "By the time I was in Grade 7, things got really bad. The same group of girls sent out a message to a large group of my classmates, saying 'Anna must die. We must get rid of her. We're sick and tired of her thinking she's better than us because she has all the boys on her side.' One girl even said we must bring a gun to school and shoot her!"

Although this sounds far-fetched in a school setting, we do know that such situations can be very real and for the person receiving such threats, really terrifying. I ask Anna if she had told anyone what was happening at the time. "I didn't say anything for quite a while, but when things became worse I did feel suicidal. Eventually my aunt noticed cuts on my arms where I'd been self-harming myself, and asked what was going on. I opened up to her and showed her the screenshots of the messages being posted. This was when my family stepped in, going to the school and asking how 13-year-old kids could be talking about shooting another girl with a gun?

"The result was the girls were called in to the principal, who told them to apologise to me – just as though they'd been nasty to me in class, not so much threatening to kill me..."

I could tell from talking to Anna that although she tries to shrug off this period in her life, it's definitely left indelible marks on her psyche. She assures me she's moved on but somehow there's still a shadow hanging over her. With no strong family ties, she's battling to handle her history alone – something no one should have to do.

A parent's role

"Part of the problem is that parents simply don't understand the issues around social media, and children know this," explains Dean McCoubrey. "I've found as a father of three girls myself that it's a case of asking questions, listening and subtly getting yourself educated. It became part of the general conversation in our home. It's vital for parents and educators to keep up with the latest technology, including artificial intelligence [AI] and augmented reality [AR], which are fast becoming a part of their children's lives. There's been a stratospheric growth trajectory in this field, which if you don't understand you can't deal with.

"In a case like Anna's, it's important for someone to explain that it's not her fault – she didn't make this happen. She shouldn't feel shame or embarrassment. This is other people who are inconsiderate and insensitive, disloyal and nasty, having what they consider fun. But to their target, it's definitely not fun. It's actually them, plus the power *and* the device. It's easy to say it shouldn't affect you, but it's the first starting point in taking off the 'cloak of shame' and saying you're an amazing human being. I can see it in your tears, in your sensitivity and openness. Despite this being impossibly difficult for you to understand, that you can come back from it – others have, and you will too.

"Yes, it sucks so badly and is incredibly painful, which is why you need to go to your parents or counsellor for support. The number one thing to remember is, it's not your fault and secondly, that you must have hope and belief that you're not alone.

"The other side of this is to teach not just children but adults to think before you post. Even when parents feel they're able to monitor their children's apps, it's still easy and inevitable that they'll simply use someone else's phone. We need to make sure that kids have some awareness – that they know they have a choice if things go wrong. They need to feel confident that there is support out there for them, because right now you're not going to stop the tsunami of social platforms," says McCoubrey.

Not just kids encounter cyberbullying

Cyberbullying can affect anyone, no matter the age – but the older the person, the less they'll want to admit it happened to them. Now with the likelihood of no parent or possibly a partner to confide in, this can become a really heavy burden.

The creepy neighbour – Sarah's story

When 40-year-old Sarah* moved into her brand-new townhouse complex she was looking forward to meeting her neighbours and hopefully finding some new friends, but what she wasn't expecting was a cyber stalker and a life filled with fear at every turn. "There were only a few of us who moved into the complex in the first few weeks, so it was easy to get to know people. When a guy who lived above me asked me to go for a coffee, I didn't think much of it other than it being a neighbourly thing to do," explains Sarah, not realising this would be the beginning of her nightmare.

"I went out twice for coffee with him and when it became obvious that he wanted more than this, I quickly put him off. But I hadn't counted on his tenacity – in the creepiest way possible. I would pull up into my parking spot at the complex and my phone would ping telling me I had a WhatsApp, and there would be a comment from him saying 'You look really good today' or 'You've been gone quite a while – did you have a good time?'"

These messages escalated in their tone, using more sexual innuendoes – sometimes not so subtle – and even though Sarah blocked him from her WhatsApp, short of changing her number or moving, he managed to appear either in person or on her timeline daily. The more she ignored him the worse it became, eventually leading to Sarah getting a restraining order against him, which of course didn't work either. As a representative of an NGO, she would often be on radio or television, which he somehow never missed. "I don't know how he did it, but he'd know I'd been on some obscure community radio station and of course message me commenting afterwards."

By now Sarah found herself continually looking over her shoulder, not just at home but wherever she went, expecting him to pop up anywhere. "Eventually I realised there was only one way to go, which was to move and change all my numbers, social media pages – everything he could get into. The day I did that I could breathe freely for the first time."

Retribution – Olivia's story

It's not just cyber stalking that can radically change your life, but just one nasty post can grow out of hand to make your everyday existence a nightmare. This was the case for Olivia* who, in her senior executive role, had no choice but to fire a junior colleague for simply not being able to carry out her duties. "I've always hated firing people, and luckily enough hadn't had to do it too often in my over 20-year career, but this time there was no other way. This woman had only been in the job a short while, so what I didn't expect was the lengths she would go to in order to try and ruin my reputation. Having a friend working for a major newspaper, she was able to get a story in there, which then of course exploded on social media.

"If this wasn't enough, the attacks became really malicious and dangerous, leading to a highly volatile situation. People threatening my kids and telling me to leave the country – the posts were absolutely vile. Despite wanting to, in one way, I didn't answer them, and in fact a colleague grabbed my phone and said he was going to delete my Twitter feed, and when he thought it was safe again he'd reload it.

"Part of these slurs around her firing was that there was a racial element to it, which was totally untrue, and luckily I had an incredible level of support and protection from my senior black colleagues and prominent black figures in my field of work. People I'd worked with over my career were incensed with this woman's rants, but that didn't stop the keyboard warriors coming out in full force," Olivia recounts.

This went on for weeks, with the perpetrator involving other people. "Six months after this started, on my birthday, I received a death threat – by SMS! They mentioned someone who had recently died that I knew, and said 'you are next, we're coming for you'. I went to the police, who said they couldn't trace the messages as they were from computer-generated phone numbers.

"What kept me sane was simply the support of my family and friends. I tried to shield my kids from what was happening but I've never been so devastated in my life. They did ask at one point why this woman was being so horrible to me. I tried to explain without scaring them, but it wasn't easy.

"When I turned to my company for support after working there for 23 years, in a very senior position, they didn't want to know my problems and weren't there for me at all. That's when I realised I couldn't stay in a company that didn't support me. To leave this job that I loved was deeply traumatic for me and the knock-on effect, several years later, still lingers.

"What has changed irrevocably is the way I communicate on social media. Nowadays I'm very conscious of sharing stories on Twitter. When something like this happens, it has a toxic ripple effect on your life – on your psyche, and both mental and physical health."

Cyberhate: a professional hazard

For some, their particular job may require that they're constantly on Twitter and other social media, highlighting issues. One such profession is of course journalism, where links to your comments and articles are now a part of the job.

One much publicised case was that of a top journalist, who mistakenly sent notes meant for the producer of her radio show, about a meeting between a political party and elders on the East Rand of Johannesburg that week, to the party's media WhatsApp group, asking them to find out "Who were these elders and were they all male?"

The WhatsApp message obviously had her cell phone number on it. Immediately, a screenshot of her message was taken and just before it was quickly deleted from the group's chat, a politician went to town reposting the screenshot on his Twitter page, which was followed by 2.3 million people. A number of the politician's followers then went on to seriously threaten her using both voice and chat messages: "You need a serious 🥒", "We're not playing here. We're dealing with racists… step aside or we will crush your prolapsed vagina" were just some of the tweets she received.

In one message, she was threatened by a meme of an image of a music producer who allegedly beat up his girlfriend. There were also many racial comments, including calling her an "Indian whore" and "bitch".

She then took this political party to the Gauteng High Court in Johannesburg, who ruled in her favour. Her response on the ruling at the time was: "A victory for media freedom, a victory against sexism and it is victory for women in journalism and protection and freedom of the media."

And she was far from the only journalist to get torched in this way. For prominent and often outspoken journalist Ferial Haffajee, knowing others disagree with what you write isn't new to her. After all, being one of South Africa's top journalists for several decades means you become accustomed to a few slings and arrows – but being stalked and receiving death threats isn't something you can easily shrug off. When I asked Ferial if I could use her story in this book, she was only too pleased to help with any initiative to help warn others about some of the darker areas of social media.

These attacks were made worse by the obvious sexist dimension they took on, at the same time pushing a new form of media censorship. In an article for *Huffington Post* entitled "Ferial, You 'Deserve a Bullet in the Head'", Haffajee comments: "Nothing beats the nasty of Twitter and social media. This wonderful tool to share, to build community and virality, has turned mean. It peddles hate and the impact is worse, in my experience, because it is so personal."[23]

The title of the article came from a DM (direct message) Haffajee received from someone named "Travor" which read: "Stop misleading pple u bitch... fuck u and go back to Europe... this is not your country asshole... u deserve a bullet in the head".

"What I didn't expect," explains Haffajee, "was that when I scrolled 'Travor's' timeline I could see a selfie of him. He didn't even bother to try and conceal his identity, which bothered me even more."

She ended her article by asking: "The hate's not even hidden any longer and it is right in our direct messages. What happens when it jumps out of the ether into the real world? And what is the responsibility of political leaders to reduce rhetoric that can inflame hate?"

With these and other less well-publicised but still horrendous invasions of privacy taking place online, it became increasingly necessary to establish guidelines of just what was and wasn't seen as breaking the law. This led, in 2015, to the Cybercrimes and Cybersecurity Bill being promulgated.

The Cybercrimes Act

However, it took until June 2021 before President Cyril Ramaphosa signed the Cybercrimes Act 19 of 2020 (as it is now known) into law. The penalties for those found guilty of breaking this law, whether organisations or individuals, consists of a fine, imprisonment (between one to fifteen years), or both. And this applies to everyone who uses a computer or the internet, as well as many other types of organisations and institutions.

Some of the offences under this act include: hacking; unlawful interception of data; use of ransomware; cyber forgery and uttering (the term used when something has been forged); cyber extortion; and malicious communications.

Tips for dealing with cyberbullying:

For adults:
- Immediately block the person harassing you, on all social media platforms.
- Keep a record of any bullying messages you receive, whether online, through messaging services such as WhatsApp, chats or voicemails. Print out anything that's likely to be taken offline.
- If any of these messages are threatening, as shown in some of the stories in this chapter, then immediately report them to the South African Police Service (SAPS) as a case of intimidation, as it may constitute imminent danger under the Intimidation Act 72 of 1982, which is defined as "situations that pose a direct and immediate danger to the individual affected by the action".

- Report the tweet/DM/post to the platform it appears on. Social media platforms have procedures in place to deal with such occurrences, and they should immediately remove the post and issue a red flag or even permanently remove the user from their platform.
- You can also get a protection order in terms of the Protection from Harassment Act 17 of 2011, if you can prove the perpetrator has harassed you and could cause you harm.
- Seek legal advice.

For minors, the same rules as above apply, plus:
- Either show a parent or teacher the messages, or make sure you keep a record or diary of all the messages, chats or voicemails.
- Try not to respond to this type of bullying. Remember, the perpetrators want to get a reaction out of you so they can continue the bullying.
- Don't start your own cyberbullying campaign against the bully, because you could find you're the one who gets into trouble.
- If someone sends you a bullying message, don't forward this on to anyone as you have no idea how far the chain can go.
- Don't believe the bully – no one deserves abusive treatment and no one should be able to hurt your self-esteem in this way, when you have done nothing to deserve it. They're cowards hiding behind their screens.

Everyone should check out the following:
- Facebook Safety Centre: https://web.facebook.com/safety
- Twitter Safety and Security: https://help.twitter.com/en/safety-and-security
- Google Safety Centre: https://safety.google/
- TikTok Safety Centre: https://www.tiktok.com/safety/en/
- Instagram Safety Tips: https://help.instagram.com/377830165708421/?helpref=hc_fnav

CONCLUSION

PERHAPS ONE OF the greatest joys I cherish as a writer is that you never stop learning, and this book was no different. *Big Bully* was born out of a desire to discover just what makes bullies tick and how people have overcome their bullying experiences – or not. So, did I learn anything new? I learnt there is no age limit or social boundary to bullying, and the effects bullying can have on an individual are lifelong. Sadly, with people becoming more and more glued to their cell phones and addicted to social media, bullying is on a fast, upward trajectory.

Many of the stories recounted truly horrified me, and as a journalist with 35 years' experience – often writing terrible stories ranging from the sex-slave trade to drugs in primary schools – that says a lot. What shook me in particular is the nonchalant way bullies churn out their abuse, whether on a school playground, within a marriage, or in the workplace. I quickly realised that bullies aren't remotely worried about the result of their actions. Only one honest teen confessed how their life was impacted when their bullying came back to haunt them, finally creating a realisation of the effect their words and deeds had caused.

Unsurprisingly, I couldn't find any "real" bullies, reformed or otherwise, who would talk to me, and even parents who have been on both sides of the bullying fence were reluctant to open up about their experiences. In several cases, when I mentioned how important this could be for parents dealing with similar situations, I could see interviewees give this deep thought, but inevitably this led to a downcast look, a shaking of the head and a profound no. This means that areas I would have liked to have gone into on a deeper level have remained untouched.

Since finishing writing the book I've been asked which area of bullying impacted me the most. This is a difficult question to answer as each section threw its own curveballs and, in some cases, horrors. I think what will shock readers the most will be how social media has impacted the vile world of bullying. What was once more obvious has now become totally invisible – hidden behind screens and read in private, few will see the misery and tears these messages and videos can bring.

With any luck, you will have found information between these pages that will help build resilience against bullying and bullies. There is no single answer or way to deal with a bully, as each situation is highly individual, but one thing all bullies have in common is that they thrive on seeing their words and actions taking effect. So doing something about it or ignoring it would seem a good strategy, but the strength to do either lies within a person and isn't easy to find alone. Talking to someone can make a real difference, and also lift some of the burden. With society and the law now becoming aware of these toxic behaviours, speaking out is even more important.

Even though we're living through massive advancements in technology and AI, the results of bullying remain the same as they have been for centuries – leaving people feeling unworthy, hurt, embarrassed, humiliated and often suicidal.

Hopefully *Big Bully* will help inform, arm and protect against this epidemic of unkindness that appears to be around every corner. Although kindness shouldn't be something we have to be taught, it's obvious there is a great need for awareness here.

If each person who reads this book can spread the word of the impact of bullying and the importance of kindness to even two or three people, the world will be a better place.

NOTES AND REFERENCES

1   Richardson, D and Hiu, CF (July 2018): *Developing a Global Indicator on Bullying of School-aged Children*. UNICEF Innocenti Working Paper. Accessed 24 January 2023. Available at: https://www.unicef-irc.org/publications/pdf/WP%202018-11.pdf

2   Byrne, B (1994): *Coping with Bullying in Schools*. Cassell, London.

3   UNESCO (1 October 2018): "New data reveal that one out of three teens is bullied worldwide". UNESCO Institute for Statistics. Accessed 24 January 2023. Available at: https://en.unesco.org/news/new-data-reveal-one-out-three-teens-bullied-worldwide

4   Adapted from: Balance Your Life (undated): "Bullying resources for parents". Accessed 23 February 2023. Available at: https://www.balanceyourlife.online/bullying-south-africa

5   According to research by privately-funded site Education.com and quoted in Lloyd, D (1 April 2012): "What happens when bullies become adults?" in *The New Bullying – Anti-bullying facts, strategies, stories and statistics by Michigan State University journalism students*. Accessed 26 January 2023. Available at: https://news.jrn.msu.edu/bullying/2012/04/01/bullies-as-adults/

6   American Psychological Association (2023): *APA Dictionary of Psychology*. Accessed 23 February 2023. Available at: https://dictionary.apa.org/narcissistic-personality-disorder

7   Cambridge University Press (2008): *Cambridge Academic Content Dictionary*. Cambridge University Press. Accessed 23 February 2023. Available at: https://dictionary.cambridge.org/dictionary/english/tease

8   Adapted from: Childline South Africa (undated): "Bullying". Accessed 31 January 2023. Available at: https://www.childlinesa.org.za/children/for-children/issues-affecting-you/bullying/

9   *Sunday World* (14 April 2021): "MEC condemns bullying video in Limpopo". Accessed 6 February 2023. Available at: https://

sundayworld.co.za/news/breaking-news/mec-condemns-bullying-video-in-limpopo/

10 Adapted from: The Olweus Bullying Prevention Group (2004): *The Bullying Circle.*

11 Department of Basic Education (2016): *Challenging Homophobic Bullying in Schools.* Accessed 8 February 2023. Available at: https://www.education.gov.za/Portals/0/Documents/Publications/Homophobic%20Bullying%20in%20Schools.pdf?ver=2016-02-19-133822-337

12 Villines, Z (26 August 2022): "What is intimate partner violence?" in *Medical News Today.* Accessed 9 February 2023. Available at: https://www.medicalnewstoday.com/articles/320747

13 Adapted from: The Centre for Relationship Abuse Awareness (undated): "What is relationship abuse?". Accessed 9 February 2023. Available at: https://stoprelationshipabuse.org/educated/what-is-relationship-abuse/

14 Ephesians 5:22, New Internationalist Version.

15 Kiecolt-Glaser, JK et al. (February 2003): "Love, marriage, and divorce: Newlyweds' stress hormones foreshadow relationship changes". *Journal of Consulting and Clinical Psychology*, 71(1):176-88. doi: 10.1037//0022-006x.71.1.176. PMID: 12602438.

16 Adapted from: CCMA Info Sheet: Harassment (2022): "Preventing and eliminating harassment in the workplace". CCMA-I832-2022-01. Accessed 14 February 2023. Available at: https://www.ccma.org.za/wp-content/uploads/2022/06/Preventing-and-Eliminating-Harassment-in-the-workplace-Info-Sheet-2022-01-1.pdf

17 Adapted from: National Health Service (undated): "Bullying at work". Accessed 14 February 2023. Available at: https://www.nhs.uk/mental-health/advice-for-life-situations-and-events/support-for-workplace-bullying/

18 We Are Social and Hootsuite (January 2022): *Digital 2022 Global Overview Report: The Essential Guide to the World's Connected Behaviours.* Accessed 14 February 2023. Available at: https://wearesocial.com/cn/wp-content/uploads/sites/8/2022/01/DataReportal-GDR002-20220126-Digital-2022-Global-Overview-Report-Essentials-v02.pdf

19 *TimesLIVE* (10 March 2021): "More than half of SA's children have been cyberbullied, survey finds". Accessed 14 February 2023. Available at: https://www.timeslive.co.za/news/south-africa/2021-03-10-more-than-half-of-sas-children-have-been-cyberbullied-survey-finds/

20 *Cape Times* (19 February 2019): "Girl, 13, commits suicide after allegedly being bullied on WhatsApp". Accessed 14 February 2023. Available at: https://www.iol.co.za/capetimes/news/girl-13-commits-suicide-after-allegedly-being-bullied-on-whatsapp-19371125

21 *Inside Edition* (1 April 2022): "Michigan teen takes his own life after explicit photo extortion plot". Accessed 14 February 2023. Available at: https://www.insideedition.com/michigan-teen-takes-his-own-life-after-explicit-photo-extortion-plot-74157

22 Walter, E (2020): *Cambridge Advanced Learner's Dictionary & Thesaurus*. Cambridge University Press. Accessed 14 February 2023. Available at: https://dictionary.cambridge.org/dictionary/english/sextortion

23 *Huffington Post* (18 June 2018): "Ferial, you 'deserve a bullet in the head'". Accessed 14 February 2023. Available at: https://www.huffingtonpost.co.uk/entry/ferial-you-deserve-a-bullet-in-the-head_uk_5c7e9c61e4b06e0d4c24c221